MW01204235

SUPERMAN VS FLASH

E. NELSON BRIDWELL
GEOFF JOHNS
DAN JURGENS
DENNY O'NEIL
MARTIN PASKO
JIM SHOOTER
WRITERS

ROSS ANDRU
RICH BURCHETT
DICK DILLIN
JOSE LUIS GARCIA-LOPEZ
DAN JURGENS
CURT SWAN
PENCILLERS

DAN ADKINS
MIKE ESPOSITO
JOE GIELLA
GEORGE KLEIN
PRENTIS ROLLINS
ART THIBERT
INKERS

JOHN COSTANZA
BEN ODA
LETTERERS

JAMES SINCLAIR
DAVID TANGUAY
GLENN WHITMORE
COLORISTS

NEAL ADAMS • JOSE LUIS GARCIA-LOPEZ & DAN ADKINS
CARMINE INFANTINO & MURPHY ANDERSON
CARMINE INFANTINO & MIKE ESPOSITO
DAN JURGENS & ART THIBERT • KEVIN NOWLAN • BOB OKSNER
ORIGINAL COVER ARTISTS

TABLE OF CONTENTS

DAN DIDIO, VP-EXECUTIVE EDITOR MIKE CARLIN, JOEY CAVALIERI, JULIUS SCHWARTZ, MORT WEISINGER, EDITORS-ORIGINAL SERIES ROBERT GREENBERGER, SENIOR EDITOR-COLLECTED EDITION ROBBIN BROSTERMAN, SENIOR ART DIRECTOR PAUL LEVITZ, PRESIDENT & PUBLISHER GEORG BREWER, VP-DESIGN & RETAIL PRODUCT DEVELOPMENT RICHARD BRUNING, SENIOR VP-CREATIVE DIRECTOR PATRICK CALDON, SENIOR VP-FINANCE & OPERATIONS CHRIS CARAMALIS, VP-FINANCE TERRI CUNNINGHAM, VP-MANAGING EDITOR STEPHANIE FIERMAN, SENIOR VP-SALES & MARKETING ALISON GILL, VP-MANUFACTURING RICH JOHNSON, VP-BOOK TRADE SALES HANK KANALZ, VP-GENERAL MANAGER, WILDSTORM LILLIAN LASERSON, SENIOR VP & GENERAL COUNSEL PAULA LOWITT, SENIOR VP-BUSINESS & LEGAL AFFAIRS JIM LEE, EDITORIAL DIRECTOR-WILDSTORM DAVID MCKILLIPS, VP-ADVERTISING & CUSTOM PUBLISHING JOHN NEE, VP-BUSINESS DEVELOPMENT GREGORY NOVECK, SENIOR VP-CREATIVE AFFAIRS CHERYL RUBIN, SENIOR VP-BRAND MANAGEMENT BOB WAYNE, VP-SALES

WHO'S FASTER?

In the 1960s, it was perfectly acceptable to sit around the newsstand and argue about the best, toughest, fastest, greatest...was having a power ring or magic lasso cooler or...who was faster, Superman or the Flash?

Little wonder, then, that teenaged comic book writer Jim Shooter was the first to write such a story in SUPERMAN #199 for editor Mort Weisinger.

"When I was a very little kid," Shooter recently recalled, "I used to draw pictures of Superman racing the Flash and imagine such a thing. The story was my idea. Mort liked it. Remember, crossovers at DC were rare-to-nonexistent in those days, so it was a breakthrough in some ways." Especially characters from different editorial offices, as was the case here.

And of course, not to denigrate either character, the race was a tie.

A rematch, in all fairness, was required, and logic dictated that FLASH host the second competition. Kid-at-heart E. Nelson Bridwell wrote that story, and once more the matter remained unresolved.

By then, readers were hooked. A winner had to be declared and a rubber match was required. Fortunately, by then, editor Julie Schwartz was converting WORLD'S FINEST into a Superman team-up title. Who better to inaugurate this than The Flash? Before you knew it, the two-part race was on and a winner finally declared.

Nearly a decade later, WORLD'S FINEST was back to featuring Superman and Batman, and Julie still liked the Superman team-up idea. His newest project, DC COMICS PRESENTS, was approved and Martin Pasko tapped as the regular writer. It seemed appropriate to once more have the race of the century and again, a winner was declared. Pasko recalls the challenge was finding a new venue for the contest when he mentioned time and Schwartz said, "Go!"

Ever since, pairing these two for a contest seemed an inevitable occurrence and for the first time, the races are collected under one cover.

SUPERMAN VS. FLASH PUBLISHED BY DC COMICS. COVER, INTRODUCTION, AND COMPILATION ORIGINALLY PUBLISHED IN SINGLE MAGAZINE FORM IN ADVENTURES OF SUPERMAN 463, DC COMICS PRESENTS 1-2, DC FIRST: FLASH/SUPERMAN, THE FLASH 175, SUPERMAN 199, WORLD'S FINEST 198-199. DC COMICS, 1700 BROADWAY, NEW YORK, NY 10019. A WARNER BROS. ENTERTAINMENT COMPANY. PRINTED IN CANADA. FIRST PRINTING. ISBN: 1-4012-0456-2 COVER ILLUSTRATION BY ALEX ROSS. COLOR RECONSTRUCTION BY DAVE TANGUAY. PUBLICATION DESIGN BY JOHN J. HILL

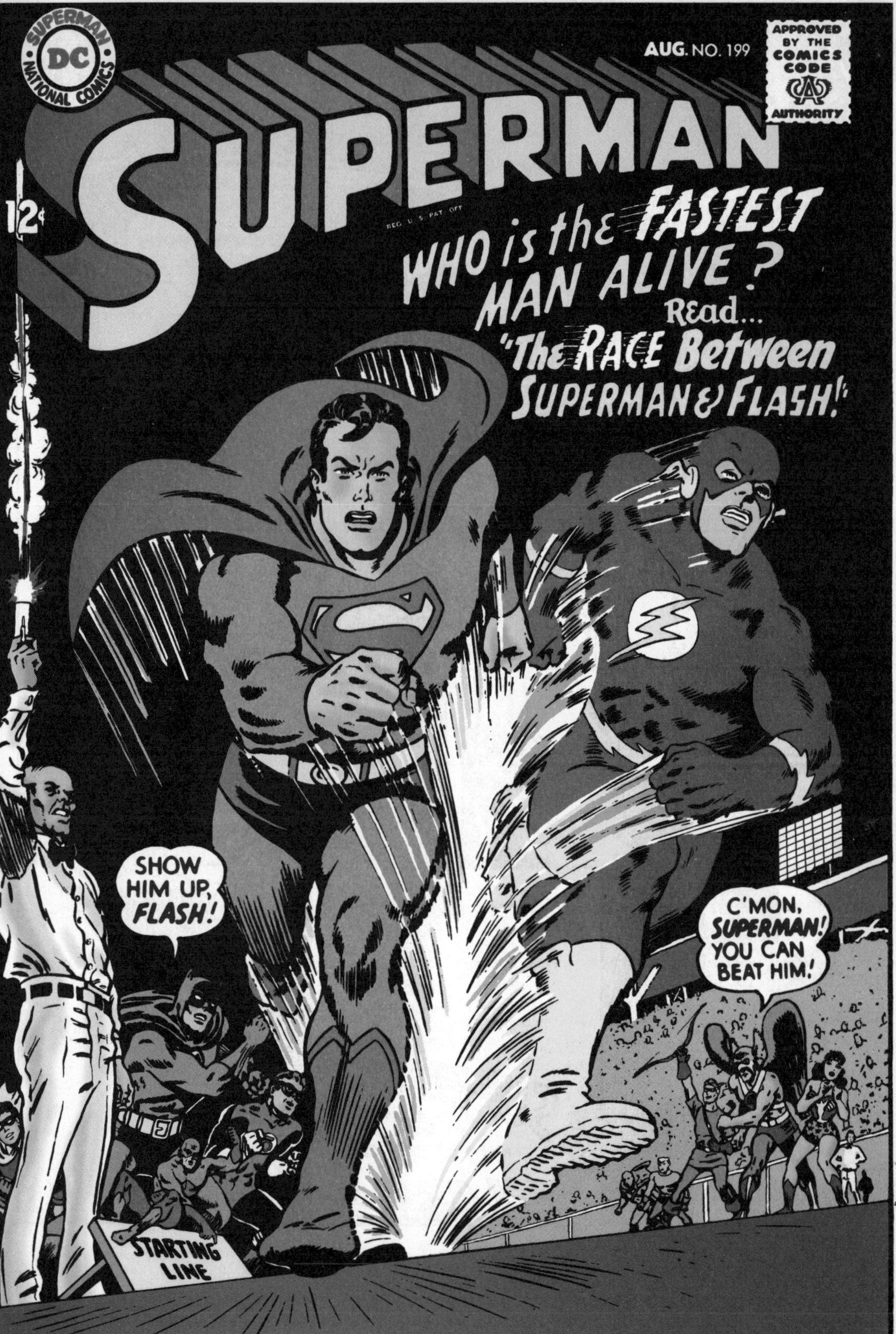
SUPERMAN
DC
NATIONAL COMICS
AUG. NO. 199
APPROVED BY THE COMICS CODE AUTHORITY
12¢
SUPERMAN
WHO is the FASTEST MAN ALIVE?
Read... "The RACE Between SUPERMAN & FLASH!"
SHOW HIM UP, FLASH!
C'MON, SUPERMAN! YOU CAN BEAT HIM!
STARTING LINE

SUPERMAN
REG. U.S. PAT. OFF.
LOOK, BOYS... OUR SYNDICATE HAS A LOTTA DOUGH RIDIN' ON SUPERMAN. SO FLASH MUST NOT WIN! HERE'S OUR PLAN...
YOU KNOW OUR SYNDICATE HAS PLENTY OF LOOT BET ON FLASH! SO SUPERMAN MUST NOT WIN! HERE'S OUR SCHEME...
PLACEMENT OF SYMBOL
COPY OF MASK
JET BOOTS
IT'S NOT OFTEN YOU FIND MOBSTERS ROOTING FOR SUPERMAN! IT'S JUST AS UNCOMMON TO HEAR HOODS CHEERING THE FLASH! BUT BOTH THESE THINGS HAPPEN WHEN TWO GAMBLING SYNDICATES SET OUT TO PUT OVER A DOUBLE-FIX IN...
SUPERMAN'S RACE WITH THE FLASH!

ONE DAY, IN METROPOLIS...
LOOK! SUPERMAN'S GOING TO SAVE THOSE CARS FROM COLLIDING!
QUICK! MY STOPWATCH!
STOPWATCH?
YES...GOT IT!... THREE-FIFTHS OF A SECOND! NOT BAD!
WHAT DO YOU MEAN, NOT BAD? WHAT'S WITH THE STOPWATCH?
CLICK!
HAVEN'T YOU HEARD?
HEARD ABOUT WHAT?
ABOUT THE RACE!

HMM! 1.5 SECONDS! OF COURSE, THERE WERE SIX OF THEM, AND HE **WASN'T** GOING AT **TOP SPEED**!

HE'S FAST, ALL RIGHT... BUT HOW DOES HE MATCH UP AGAINST **SUPERMAN**?

WE'LL SEE NEXT WEEK!

NEXT WEEK? YOU MEAN THEY'VE SET THE DATE?

LOOK FOR YOURSELF! THEY JUST PUT UP THAT SIGN!

The FLASH Vs. SUPERMAN THE GREATEST RACE OF ALL TIME SAT. JUNE 10TH

SUPERMAN VERSUS **FLASH**! MAN, THAT'S GONNA BE THE RACE OF THE CENTURY!

*HOLD IT, READER! WE KNOW THE QUESTION SPINNING THROUGH YOUR MIND! HOW DID THIS TURN OF EVENTS COME ABOUT? FOR THE ANSWER LET'S GO BACK IN TIME TWO WEEKS, TO THE OFFICE OF THE **UNITED NATIONS SECRETARY-GENERAL**...*

GREETINGS, GENTLEMEN! COME IN!

I CALLED YOU HERE TO MAKE AN IMPORTANT REQUEST OF YOU!
WE'LL BE GLAD TO HELP THE U.N. IN ANY WAY, SIR!
GOOD! THEN YOU WILL NOT MIND RUNNING A RACE?

A RACE??
YES! YOU SEE, OUR CAMPAIGN FOR FUNDS TO AID UNDER-DEVELOPED COUNTRIES IS FALLING FAR SHORT OF ITS MARK! WE NEED MONEY FOR SCHOOLS, HOSPITALS, FOOD AND CLOTHING FOR POVERTY-STRICKEN LANDS! A WORLD-WIDE SWEEPSTAKES, BASED ON A RACE BETWEEN YOU TWO, COULD SOLVE OUR PROBLEM!
3

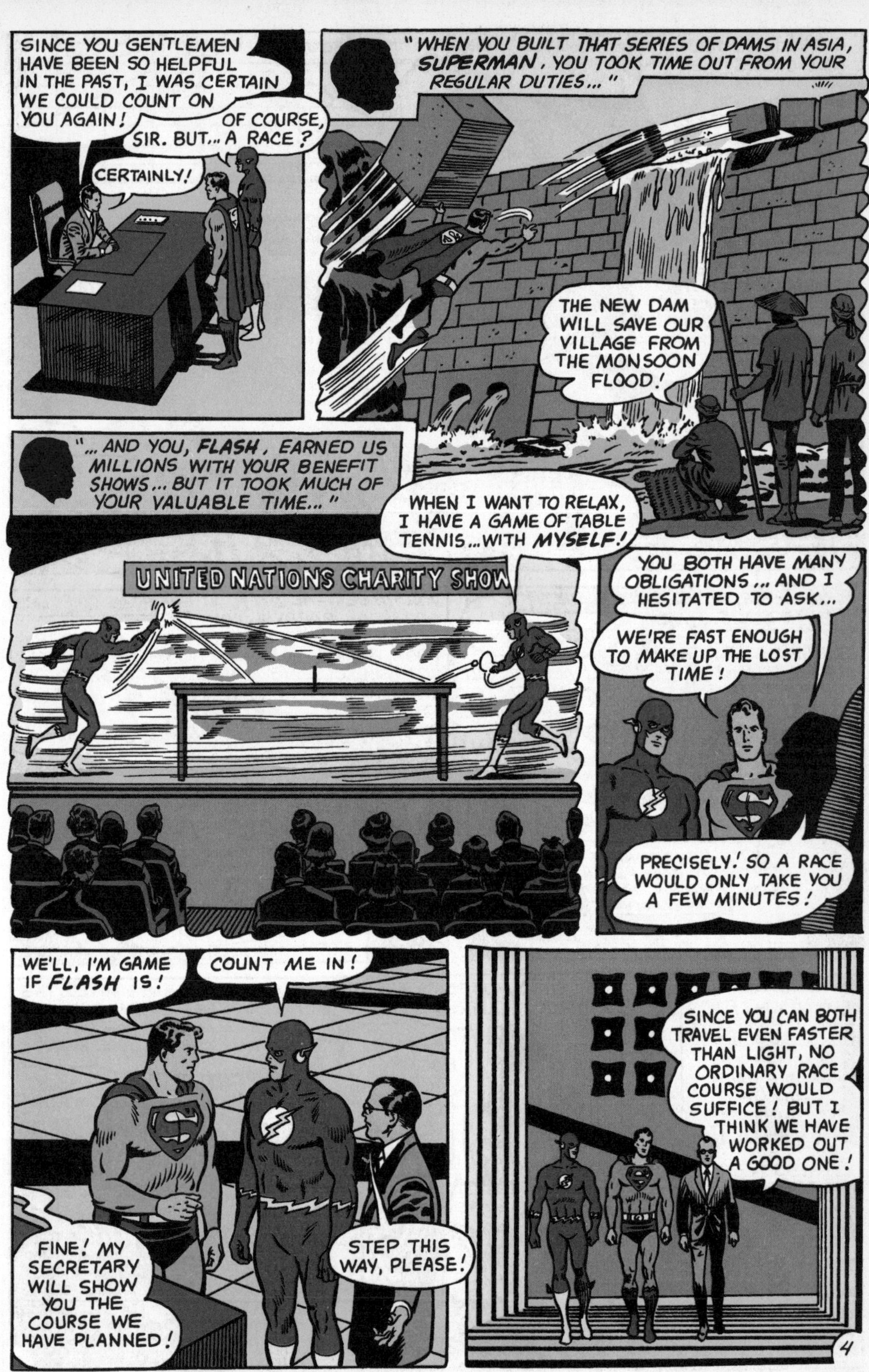
SINCE YOU GENTLEMEN HAVE BEEN SO HELPFUL IN THE PAST, I WAS CERTAIN WE COULD COUNT ON YOU AGAIN!
OF COURSE, SIR. BUT... A RACE?
CERTAINLY!
"WHEN YOU BUILT THAT SERIES OF DAMS IN ASIA, SUPERMAN, YOU TOOK TIME OUT FROM YOUR REGULAR DUTIES..."
THE NEW DAM WILL SAVE OUR VILLAGE FROM THE MONSOON FLOOD!
"... AND YOU, FLASH, EARNED US MILLIONS WITH YOUR BENEFIT SHOWS... BUT IT TOOK MUCH OF YOUR VALUABLE TIME..."
WHEN I WANT TO RELAX, I HAVE A GAME OF TABLE TENNIS... WITH MYSELF!
UNITED NATIONS CHARITY SHOW
YOU BOTH HAVE MANY OBLIGATIONS... AND I HESITATED TO ASK...
WE'RE FAST ENOUGH TO MAKE UP THE LOST TIME!
PRECISELY! SO A RACE WOULD ONLY TAKE YOU A FEW MINUTES!
WE'LL, I'M GAME IF FLASH IS!
COUNT ME IN!
FINE! MY SECRETARY WILL SHOW YOU THE COURSE WE HAVE PLANNED!
STEP THIS WAY, PLEASE!
SINCE YOU CAN BOTH TRAVEL EVEN FASTER THAN LIGHT, NO ORDINARY RACE COURSE WOULD SUFFICE! BUT I THINK WE HAVE WORKED OUT A GOOD ONE!
4

HERE IT IS! YOU WILL CIRCLE THE EARTH THREE TIMES... EACH TIME ON A SLIGHTLY *DIFFERENT* ROUTE! UNDER NORMAL CONDITIONS, IT WOULD TAKE YOU *LESS* THAN A *SECOND!*

HOWEVER, THESE PATHS HAVE BEEN SPECIALLY SELECTED FOR THE *OBSTACLES* THEY INCLUDE, WHICH SHOULD MAKE THINGS MORE *INTERESTING,* AS THAT 3-D SIMULATION SUGGESTS!

SOON AFTER, AT THE DAILY PLANET, IN METROPOLIS...
TERRIFIC STORY, CLARK! I WANT YOU TO COVER THE RACE!
WILL DO, PERRY!
AND I'LL GET THE FACTS FIRST-HAND... AS SUPERMAN!
DAILY PLANET
SUPERMAN TO RACE FLASH FOR U.N. BENEFIT BY CLARK KENT
AND IN CENTRAL CITY, AT THE HOME OF POLICE SCIENTIST BARRY ALLEN...
LOOK, BARRY... I GOT AN EXCLUSIVE INTERVIEW WITH THE FLASH!
NICE GOING, HONEY!
WOULD IRIS BE SURPRISED IF SHE KNEW HER HUSBAND WAS THE FLASH!
PICTURE NEWS
IS FLASH FASTEST MAN ALIVE? RACE WITH SUPERMAN TO PROVIDE ANSWER
STORY BY IRIS ALLEN

AND NOW, BACK TO THE PRESENT, WHERE THE EXCITEMENT GROWS EACH MINUTE...
EVERYBODY IN METROPOLIS IS TALKING ABOUT THE RACE!
WHO DO YOU THINK WILL WIN?
NOBODY'S EVER OUTRUN FLASH!
ME, I'M BACKING SUPIE!
HANDICAPPERS
THE U.N. HAS LIMITED THE NUMBER OF SWEEPSTAKES TICKETS ANYONE CAN BUY, SO NO ONE CAN LOSE MUCH!
GOOD IDEA!
5

BUT IT ISN'T ONLY THE HOLDERS OF SWEEPSTAKES TICKETS WHO ARE INTERESTED IN THE RACE'S OUTCOME... FOR, IN THE AJAX IMPORT COMPANY BUILDING, FRONT FOR AMERICA'S TOP GAMBLING SYNDICATE...
GOOD NEWS FROM OUR MAN IN PARIS... THE EUROPEAN SYNDICATE HAS COVERED OUR BET OF ONE BILLION DOLLARS ON SUPERMAN!
WHEW! WHOEVER LOSES THAT GAMBLE GETS A ONE-WAY TICKET TO THE POOR HOUSE!

HE'S RIGHT, MR. VINCENT! IF SUPERMAN BLOWS THE RACE, OUR ORGANIZATION GOES BANKRUPT!
SO WE MUST MAKE SURE SUPERMAN DOES NOT LOSE!
YOU MEAN... A FIX?

PRECISELY! MEET DR. WERNER VON BRODER! HE WILL SHOW YOU HOW WE'LL PULL THE SYNDICATE'S GREATEST COUP!
VON BRODER! ONLY LUTHOR IS A GREATER CRIMINAL SCIENTIST! WE CAN'T LOSE!

NOW LET'S LOOK IN ON ENTERPRISES INTERNATIONAL DE EUROPE, WHICH IS REALLY THE CONTINENTAL CRIME SYNDICATE...
OUR FOOLISH AMERICAN RIVALS WILL SOON BE OUT OF BUSINESS! THE FLASH WILL WIN... AND WE WILL COLLECT BILLIONS OF FRANCS!
BUT MONSIEUR DE PAUL... HOW CAN YOU BE SURE?

BECAUSE I HAVE ENGAGED DR. ROBERT CARSON, THE FAMED CRIMINAL INVENTOR, TO MAKE SURE!
AH! THE AMERICANS ARE AS GOOD AS BEATEN!
6

FINALLY, A WEEK LATER, THE PERIOD FOR GAMBLING, LEGAL OR OTHERWISE, IS PAST, AND THE TIME OF DECISION ARRIVES...
HOLY COW! THIS PLACE IS LIKE A SUPER-HEROES' CONVENTION! LOOK... THE WHOLE JUSTICE LEAGUE!
GET THAT CAMERA IN CLOSER!
YAY-SUPERMAN
I GOT MY PROGRAM AUTOGRAPHED BY BOTH OF THEM ... AT SUPER-SPEED!
GROOVY!
HOORAY FOR FLASH!

GOOD LUCK, FLASH!
WE'LL BE WAITING FOR YOU IN THE WINNER'S CIRCLE!
SHOW HIM YOUR BEST, SUPERMAN!
HOLY WESTERN UNION! LOOK AT ALL THE TELEGRAMS!

SUPERMAN! FLASH! WE WANT YOU TO GO OVER THE RULES ONCE MORE FOR THE CAMERAS! THEN --ON TO THE STARTING LINE!
WELL, THIS IS IT, FLASH! GOOD LUCK!
SAME TO YOU, SUPERMAN!

THIS WILL BE A FOOTRACE, SO YOU, SUPERMAN, CANNOT FLY! EITHER OF YOU COULD CIRCLE THE EARTH MANY TIMES IN A SECOND, SO YOUR SPEED WILL BE LIMITED! YOUR SKILL IN USING IT WILL BE THE DETERMINING FACTOR!

READY...ON YOUR MARKS...
AT THE SOUND OF THE GUN...
7

BANG
OFFICIAL
GO!
WITH INCREDIBLE VELOCITY, THE TWO SPEEDSTERS THUNDER ALONG THE SPECTATOR-LINED STREETS...
...AND TOWARDS THE DOCKS, WHERE THE SUPER-MARATHON BEGINS IN EARNEST...
RNER
MARY
MEANWHILE, BACK AT THE STARTING POINT, THE OTHER HEROES WATCH ON A MONITOR CREATED BY GREEN LANTERN'S POWER RING...
WELL, ONCE THEY REACH THE WATER, IT'LL BE CLEAR SAILING!
EXCEPT FOR THE OBSTACLES WE'VE PLANNED!
YOU HAVE US ALL IN SUSPENSE! EVEN WE DON'T KNOW WHAT THE OBSTACLES ARE!
AND IN THE HARBOR...
THERE THEY GO! THEY'RE HEADING ACROSS THE ATLANTIC FOR AFRICA!
8

AS THE TWO RAPIDLY LEAVE AMERICA FAR BEHIND THE HORIZON ...
FLASH CAN RUN ON THE WATER'S SURFACE...BUT I CAN TOP HIM BY SWIMMING WITH SUPER-STRENGTH THROUGH THE WAVES HE HAS TO GO OVER!

AND SO, WITHIN SECONDS, THE VIZIER OF VELOCITY AND THE SUPER-SULTAN OF SPEED APPROACH THE COAST OF AFRICA AT 140,000 MILES AN HOUR...

LOOK! THEY'RE HERE!
KEEP THE CAMERAS ON THEM! GET A SHOT OF THEM RACING THROUGH THE VILLAGE!
HOW? THEY'RE ALREADY GONE!

ONE SECOND LATER, APPROACHING THE ALGERIAN SAHARA...
WE'RE NEARING THE OUTSKIRTS OF THE DESERT... THE FIRST MAJOR OBSTACLE...

FLASH HAS TAKEN THE LEAD BY VIBRATING THE MOLECULES OF HIS BODY SO HE CAN PASS RIGHT THROUGH THE SAND DUNES, WHILE I MUST BORE THROUGH!
9

SOON...
MY AURA PROTECTS ME FROM THE HEAT OF AIR FRICTION, BUT NOT FROM THESE SCORCHING-HOT SAND DUNES! I MUST SLOW DOWN... COOL OFF!
FLASH IS FALLING BACK!
BUT SECONDS LATER, AS THE TWO RACERS SPEED TOWARD GIZEH, IN EGYPT!
THE GREAT PYRAMID OF CHEOPS. FLASH VIBRATED THROUGH, WHILE I HAD TO GO OVER THE TOP! WE'RE EVEN AGAIN!
LOOK! THEY ENTER THE VILLAGE!
THE PATH HAS BEEN CLEARED THROUGH THE MARKET SQUARE! EVERYONE WILL BE WATCHING!
WELL, ALMOST EVERYONE...
THAT MERCHANT... DRIVING HIS CART ACROSS THE SQUARE! WE CAN'T AVOID HITTING HIM!
AIEEE!
MY FIGS! MY CART!
10

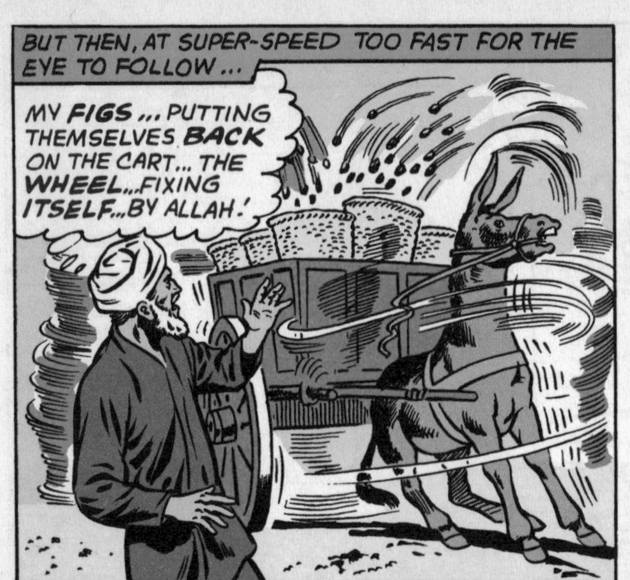
BUT THEN, AT SUPER-SPEED TOO FAST FOR THE EYE TO FOLLOW...
MY FIGS... PUTTING THEMSELVES BACK ON THE CART... THE WHEEL...FIXING ITSELF...BY ALLAH!

AND SO, THE DAMAGE RECTIFIED, THE MONARCHS OF MOTION RESUME THEIR CONTEST...
AIEEEE! SAVE ME! THE MARKET IS HAUNTED!

AND SO THE RACE OF THE HEROES CONTINUES...THROUGH THE RED SEA... ACROSS THE SANDY WASTELANDS OF SAUDI ARABIA AND IRAQ...THE ARID HIGHLANDS OF IRAN AND AFGHANISTAN...

AND FINALLY... TO THE HIMALAYAS...
I WONDER HOW FLASH IS HOLDING UP IN THIS CHILLY AIR AT HIS REDUCED SPEED?
EVEN I WOULD BE SLOWED UP IF I TRIED TO VIBRATE CLEAR THROUGH THIS HUGE RANGE... BUT THE RAREFIED AIR AND INTENSE COLD CUT MY SPEED, ANYWAY! HERE'S WHERE SUPERMAN'S INVULNERABILITY GIVES HIM THE EDGE!
11

SOON, HOWEVER, THE INTENSE COLD IS LEFT BEHIND, AS THE FLASH AND SUPERMAN RACE SOUTHWARD TO INDIA'S FERTILE COASTAL PLAIN...
WE'VE GONE THROUGH LUCKNOW AND BENARES..., NOW WE'RE SUPPOSED TO PASS THROUGH THE PORT OF CALCUTTA, THEN FOLLOW THE GANGES RIVER TO THE BAY OF BENGAL!

SECONDS LATER...
LOOK! ONE OF THEM RUNS ON THE WATERS!
AND THE OTHER SWIMS WITH THE SPEED OF LIGHTNING!

BY BUDDHA! THEY COME!
FIRST, THEY WILL PASS THROUGH THE JUNGLE!
THEN TURN SOUTHWARD TO RANGOON!

IN THE DENSE FOREST, AS TWO BLURRED FIGURES RACE AT FANTASTIC SPEED ALONG AN ELEPHANT TRAIL...
THERE'S A TEAKWOOD LUMBER CAMP AHEAD! WONDER IF FLASH IS THINKING THE SAME THING I AM?

YEP! AS LONG AS WE'RE HERE, WE MIGHT AS WELL MAKE OURSELVES USEFUL, BY GIVING THESE BURMESE LUMBERJACKS A HAND!
MY SUPER-SPEED GIVES ME ENOUGH MOMENTUM TO SLICE THROUGH THESE TREE TRUNKS!
LOOK! OUR LUMBER QUOTA FOR TOMORROW IS FILLED!
12
THERE'S NO TIME TO TAKE A REST NOW. THE RACE CONTINUES IMMEDIATELY IN PART II!

PART II "FASTER THAN A SPEEDING BULLET"
MEANWHILE, ON THE OTHER SIDE OF THE WORLD...
THIS IS BRET BRADLEY IN METROPOLIS! I HAVE THE LATEST REPORT ON THE GREAT SUPERMAN—FLASH RACE! THEY WERE LAST SEEN IN THE FORESTS OF BURMA, BUT...
...EVEN AS I AM SPEAKING, THEY HAVE CROSSED THAILAND AND ARE NOW IN THE SOUTH CHINA SEA...
CHINA
PACIFIC OCEAN
BURMA
RANGOON
THAILAND
VIETNAM
PHILIPPINE REPUBLIC
GULF OF SIAM
MALAYA
INDONESIA

AND IN THE CHINA SEA, WHERE A U.S. PATROL BOAT SPEEDS TOWARDS THE COURSE OF THE RACING HEROES...
WE MUST INTERCEPT THE FLASH!

BUT...
TOO LATE! THERE THEY GO!
THEN...WE CAN'T WARN FLASH...ABOUT THE TYPHOON!

TOO LATE!...BUT DON'T WORRY... FLASH WILL FIND OUT FOR HIMSELF ...SOON ENOUGH...
THE WAVES ARE GETTING HIGH...ROUGH! THE WINDS ARE AT HURRICANE FORCE... IT'S GETTING HARDER TO STAY ON THE SURFACE!
FLASH IS IN TROUBLE! EVEN HE CAN'T KEEP HIS BALANCE IN THIS RAGING SEA!
13

SUDDENLY...
OHH!
FLASH DIDN'T SPOT THAT WAVE! HE'S STUNNED! THE NEXT ONE WILL FINISH HIM...

...UNLESS I GIVE HIM A LIFT WITH MY SUPER-BREATH! HE'LL THINK THE POWERFUL WINDS DID IT!
IF HE FELT INDEBTED TO ME, HE MIGHT NOT GO ALL OUT TO WIN!

AND SO, THE TWO SUPER-FIGURES SPEED ACROSS THE TURBULENT WATERS OF THE **CHINA SEA**, THROUGH THE **PHILIPPINES**, AND FINALLY TO THE CALM, WARM BILLOWS OF THE **PACIFIC**...

...WHERE EACH ISLAND WAY-STATION GREETS THEM IN ITS OWN UNIQUE MANNER...
ALOHA! FLASH-SUPERMAN HAWAII

AND BACK IN THE **U.S.**, WHERE THE REST OF THE **J. L. A.** MEMBERS WAIT ANXIOUSLY...

MY MARTIAN HEARING DETECTS THE CHEERS AS THEY APPROACH **ACAPULCO, MEXICO.**

THEY'RE GOING MUCH **FASTER** THAN **SOUND!** MY POWER RING SHOWS THEY'RE **ALREADY** IN **COLOMBIA!**

MEANWHILE, IN THE COLOMBIAN ANDES...
TOLIMA... THE VOLCANO... IN ONE OF ITS ERUPTIVE SPASMS! EH? WHAT'S THAT FLYING OUT OF THE CRATER?
14

IT'S KRYPTONITE...THE ONE SUBSTANCE DEADLY TO SUPERMAN! IT'S ALREADY WEAKENED HIM! IT MAY KILL HIM... UNLESS I DO SOMETHING!

AH! BY VIBRATING MY FEET, I'VE OPENED A FISSURE IN THE ROCK! THE GREEN K IS TUMBLING IN...SUPERMAN WILL THINK A VOLCANIC TREMOR CAUSED IT! NOW HE WON'T FEEL INDEBTED TO ME!

AND SO, SECONDS LATER, THE TWO RACE DOWN THROUGH THE PERUVIAN HIGHLANDS, ONTO THE BRAZILIAN MATTO GROSSO...

WHEN THE TWO SPEEDSTERS REACH A DEEP, WIDE CHASM...
I'M FORBIDDEN TO FLY, BUT THERE ARE NO RULES AGAINST A SUPER-LEAP!
THE ONLY "BRIDGE" IN THE AREA IS THESE TELEPHONE LINES...SO I'LL PERFORM THE WORLD'S FASTEST WIRE-WALKING ACT!

NEXT, ACROSS THE ATLANTIC, TO GABON, IN AFRICA...
THERE'S THE BEACON! THAT'S WHERE WE'RE SUPPOSED TO ENTER THE JUNGLE!

AND DEEP IN THE INTERIOR OF THE CONTINENT...
LISTEN! THE DRUMS! THE HEROES HAVE BEEN SEEN! WATCH AS THEY PASS THROUGH THE VILLAGE, SO I CAN RADIO WHO IS AHEAD TO BRAZZAVILLE!
15

LOOK! **FLASH** LEADS!

THE DENSE UNDERGROWTH WHICH **FLASH** CAN VIBRATE THROUGH SLOWS **ME** UP! BUT JUST AHEAD THERE'S AN OBSTACLE I'LL GAIN FROM!

VICTORIA FALLS, TANZANIA! I CAN SWIM RIGHT **DOWN** THE FALLS WITHOUT SLACKENING MY SPEED, BUT **FLASH** HAS TO DESCEND SLOWLY, VIBRATING HIS FEET TO BUILD UP AN AIR PRESSURE CUSHION TO BREAK HIS FALL!

MEANWHILE, HALFWAY AROUND THE WORLD, IN THE HEADQUARTERS OF THE **AMERICAN GAMBLING SYNDICATE...**

BOSS, **FLASH** CAUGHT UP TO **SUPERMAN** AGAIN IN THE JUNGLES PAST THE FALLS! NOW THEY'RE HALFWAY ACROSS THE **INDIAN OCEAN!**

GOOD! WHEN THEY START THE FINAL LAP, SOUND THE **READY ALERT!**

SOON, IN SASKATCHEWAN, CANADA...
FROZEN LAKES... HUNDREDS OF THEM IN THIS AREA! THEIR SLIPPERY SURFACE MIGHT BE AN OBSTACLE, BUT MY SUPER-BALANCE MAKES THEM AN ADVANTAGE! I CAN SLIDE AS FAST AS I CAN RUN! HMM! FLASH DOESN'T SEEM TO BE DOING AS WELL!
THIS IS AS BAD AS FIGHTING CAPT. COLD! ...CAN'T GET ANY TRACTION ...SLIPPING ALL OVER THE PLACE!

SUDDENLY...
WHA...? UHHH!
FLASH!
HE'S OUT COLD! HE MAY BE INJURED! I CAN'T JUST LEAVE HIM HERE... AND IF I STOP TO HELP, I COULD HURT HIS PRIDE!

SO, MINUTES LATER...
OH-H! MY HEAD! WHAT HAPPENED? WHO ARE YOU?
I'M CLARK KENT, A REPORTER! I WAS COVERING YOUR RACE THROUGH CANADA BY HELICOPTER, WHEN I SAW YOU FALL!

SOON...
THANKS, KENT! ANYTIME YOU WANT AN INTERVIEW, JUST WHISTLE!
I'LL REMEMBER THAT! BYE, FLASH!
NOW TO SWITCH TO SUPERMAN AND RETURN THESE PARKAS TO THE HUNTING LODGE I BORROWED THEM FROM!

SECONDS LATER, IN THE NORTH ATLANTIC, THE MAN OF STEEL DRAWS UP ALONGSIDE HIS OPPONENT...
FLASH SEEMS FULLY RECOVERED! GOOD! WE'LL BE NECK AND NECK WHEN WE REACH THE NEXT OBSTACLE!
17

ICEBERGS! THESE WILL NEVER MENACE SHIPPING LANES AGAIN!
THERE'S THE MARK OF A HERO! I HAVE TO SMASH THROUGH THESE BERGS ANYWAY, BUT FLASH, WHO COULD VIBRATE THROUGH, IS HELPING ME CRACK THEM APART!

MEANWHILE, IN THE GREAT CENTRAL STATION, IN METROPOLIS...
THE LATEST NEWS FROM OUR CORRESPONDENTS ON THE CONTINENT IS THAT SUPERMAN AND THE FLASH HAVE PASSED THROUGH SPAIN AND FRANCE, AND ARE NOW IN WEST GERMANY, STILL NECK AND NECK!
INFORMATION
INFO

AND, JUST OUTSIDE MUNICH...
OH, NO! A LONG FREIGHT TRAIN CROSSING AHEAD! FLASH CAN VIBRATE THROUGH... BUT WHAT CAN I DO? I'M NOT ALLOWED TO FLY OVER!

SO...
WELL, IF I'M DENIED MY WAY OF DOING IT, I'LL JUST PULL ANOTHER LEAF FROM FLASH'S BOOK AND RUN UP ONE SIDE AND DOWN THE OTHER!

THEN, AT 140 MILES A SECOND, THE TWO SUPER-SPEEDSTERS THUNDER ACROSS CZECHOSLOVAKIA, POLAND AND THE SPRAWLING SOVIET UNION, DRAWING EVER NEARER TO THE END OF THEIR MONUMENTAL RACE...
18

WHILE IN THE HEADQUARTERS OF THE AMERICAN SYNDICATE...
LOOK, BOSS! THEY'RE ISLAND-HOPPING THE ALEUTIANS!
GOOD, GOOD! IT WON'T BE LONG NOW!

AND AT THE EUROPEANS' AMERICAN BASE...
NOW THEY ARE HEADING ALONG THE COAST... TOWARDS SAN FRANCISCO...
SOON, SOON...

MOMENTS LATER, IN SAN FRANCISCO BAY...
LOOK! THEY'RE PASSING UNDER THE GOLDEN GATE BRIDGE!
NOW FOR THE LAST LEG OF OUR JOURNEY...ACROSS THE CONTINENT ON THE LINCOLN HIGHWAY!

AT THAT MOMENT, ON A DESERTED STRETCH OF PAVEMENT IN NEVADA...
NOW! LOWER THE GLASS PLATE ACROSS FLASH'S HALF OF THE ROAD! HE'LL BE HERE IN SECONDS AT THE RATE HE'S TRAVELING!

AND A FEW MILES DOWN THE ROAD...
NOW! SPRAY THE DUST ACROSS SUPERMAN'S HALF OF THE HIGHWAY!

THEN...
HERE THEY COME!
GOOD! EVERYTHING IS READY!
19

THEN, WITH EAR-SHATTERING IMPACT, A CAREENING FLASH CRASHES INTO A HUGE PANEL OF BULLET-PROOF GLASS, TOO TRANSPARENT FOR HIM TO SEE IN TIME TO VIBRATE THROUGH...
AND SUPERMAN, SPEEDING TOO FAST TO SPOT HIS FRIENDLY FOE'S PREDICAMENT, RUNS HEADLONG INTO THE KRYPTONITE DUST TRAP OF THE EUROPEAN SYNDICATE A FEW MILES AWAY...
WE'VE DONE IT! WE'VE CAPTURED THE FLASH!
WOW! HE WAS REALLY TRAVELING! HE ACTUALLY SMASHED THROUGH THE GLASS AND THE IMPACT KNOCKED HIM OUT!
AND DOWN THE ROAD...
SUCCESS! SUPERMAN IS OUR PRISONER!
BUT WHERE IS THE FLASH? I DID NOT SEE HIM RACE BY!
FOOL! HE WAS RUNNING TOO FAST TO BE SEEN!
PUT SUPERMAN WHERE HE WILL BE SAFE... WITH SOME KRYPTONITE GAS TURNED ON HIM!
LORENZO, MY SPANISH FRIEND... WITH YOUR COSTUME, MAKE-UP, AND ROCKET BOOTS, YOU CAN PASS FOR SUPERMAN... AND LOSE THE RACE!
SI!
20

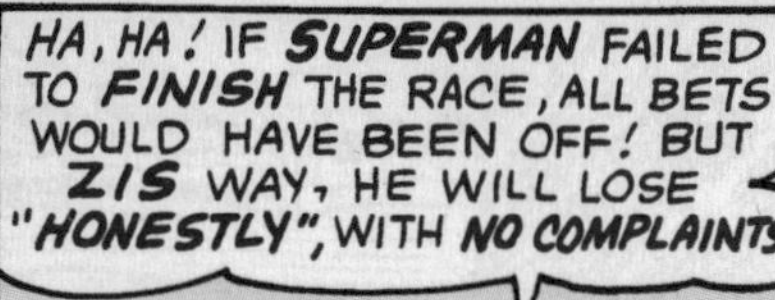
HA, HA! IF SUPERMAN FAILED TO FINISH THE RACE, ALL BETS WOULD HAVE BEEN OFF! BUT ZIS WAY, HE WILL LOSE "HONESTLY", WITH NO COMPLAINTS.

AND A FEW MILES BACK...
GET GOING, "NAILS"! AND REMEMBER... WHEN YOU LOSE, DON'T MAKE ANY EXCUSES! THEN WE COLLECT A COOL BILLION!
GOTCHA, BOSS! THESE JET BOOTS MAKE ME GO LIKE FLASH, ONLY SLOWER.

...AND SPEAKING OF FLASH, OUR SLEEPY FRIEND IS WAKING UP!
THOSE SPECIAL ROPES WILL TIGHTEN IF YOU TRY TO VIBRATE FREE!

BUT WAIT... WHAT OF THE JLA MEMBERS WHO ARE MONITORING THE RACE?
THE SCREEN'S BLANK! WHAT HAPPENED TO THE PICTURE, GL?
APPARENTLY THE HEAT OF THE NEVADA DESERT FORMED A YELLOWISH HAZE! ANYTHING YELLOW AFFECTS MY POWER RING!

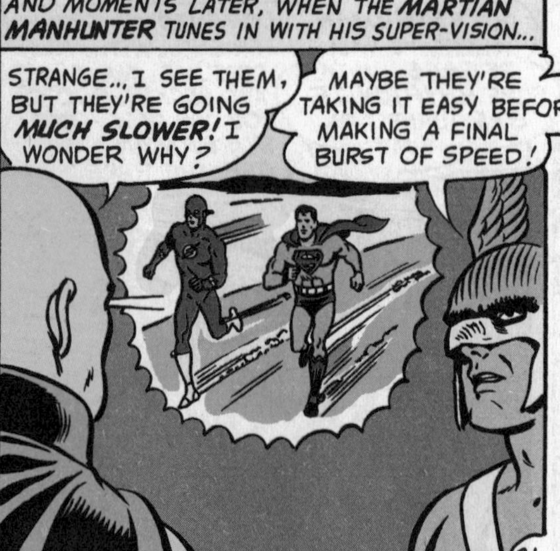
AND MOMENTS LATER, WHEN THE MARTIAN MANHUNTER TUNES IN WITH HIS SUPER-VISION...
STRANGE... I SEE THEM, BUT THEY'RE GOING MUCH SLOWER! I WONDER WHY?
MAYBE THEY'RE TAKING IT EASY BEFORE MAKING A FINAL BURST OF SPEED!
21

MEANWHILE...
THE FLASH WILL EASILY DEFEAT YOUR STAND-IN! AND WE WILL BE A BILLION DOLLARS RICHER!
WILL THEY? MY TELESCOPIC VISION REVEALS THAT HIS AMERICAN RIVALS HAVE PULLED THE SAME STUNT!
'K' GAS

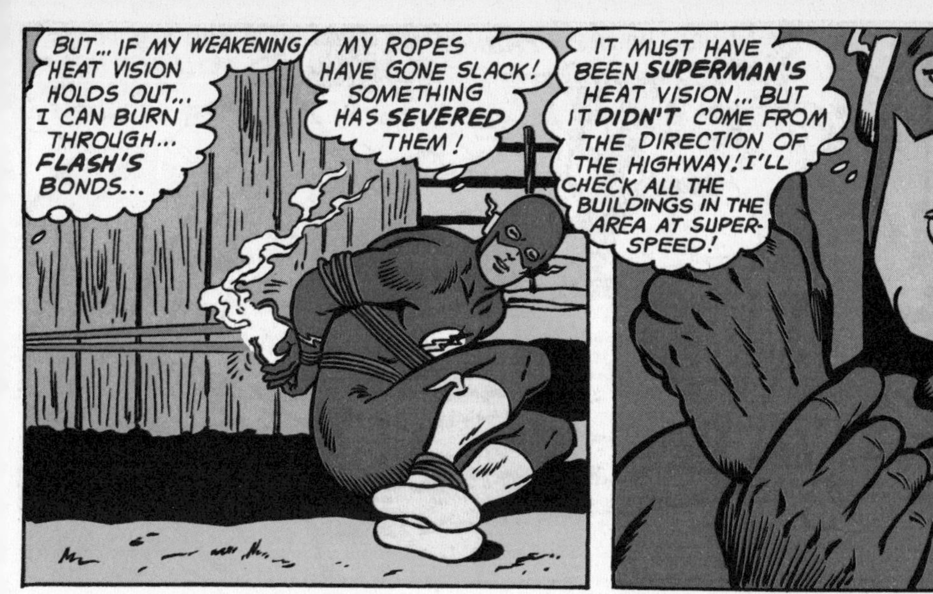
BUT... IF MY WEAKENING HEAT VISION HOLDS OUT... I CAN BURN THROUGH... FLASH'S BONDS...
MY ROPES HAVE GONE SLACK! SOMETHING HAS SEVERED THEM!
IT MUST HAVE BEEN SUPERMAN'S HEAT VISION... BUT IT DIDN'T COME FROM THE DIRECTION OF THE HIGHWAY! I'LL CHECK ALL THE BUILDINGS IN THE AREA AT SUPER-SPEED!

A FEW SECONDS LATER...
EH? SOMETHING ZOOMED BY AND KNOCKED THAT TANK OF KRYPTONITE GAS OVER, JAMMING THE VALVE! FLASH FOUND ME!

AND NOW, GENTLEMEN...
HUH? SUPERMAN! GULP! HE'S FREE!

AND AT THE OTHER GAMBLING LAIR...
PARDON ME... CAN YOU DIRECT ME TO THE FINISH LINE?
SACRE BLEU! FLASH! GULP!

MEANWHILE, LET'S CATCH UP WITH THE IMPOSTORS...
I DON'T GET IT! WHY ISN'T SUPERMAN BEATING ME? I'D BETTER PUT ON THE BRAKES!
CARAMBA! FLASH IS SLOWING DOWN! BUT HE IS SUPPOSED TO WIN! I MUST GO STILL SLOWER!
22

SOON, THE INEVITABLE HAPPENS, AND BOTH "RINGERS" COME TO A DEAD STOP...
HEY! YOU'RE A PHONEY!
AND I SUPPOSE YOU ARE NOT A FRAUD, EH, SEÑOR?

LOOK, BUD! I DON'T KNOW WHAT YOU'RE DOIN' IN THAT GET-UP, BUT YOU'RE GONNA START RUNNIN' AND YOU'RE GONNA WIN THIS RACE, SEE?
SAYS WHO, AMIGO?
WHOOOOOOO
ME! NOW GET RUNNIN', OR ELSE!
WAIT... WHAT IS THAT NOISE!

THE FLASH!
SUPERMAN!
EYAH-A-A!

AND SO, ONCE AGAIN, THE TWO FIGURES BLAZE ACROSS THIS GREAT LAND TOWARD THE FINISH LINE...

WITH EVERY STEP THAT BRINGS THEM CLOSER TO THEIR GOAL, THEIR PACE **INCREASES** AND THEIR DETERMINATION GROWS STRONGER...

BREATHLESS CROWDS LINE THE LAST MILES OF HIGHWAY, ANXIOUS TO SEE THE SUPERHUMAN ANTAGONISTS AS THEY RACE DOWN THE **FINAL STRETCH ...**
SUPERMAN

TO THE MOMENT OF DECISION...
FINISH
THE FLASH
SUPERMAN
WE BROKE THE TAPE **SIMULTANEOUSLY,** JUST AS WE PLANNED! SINCE **NEITHER** OF US WON, NONE OF THE GAMBLERS CAN COLLECT!
IT'S A **TIE!**
METTV

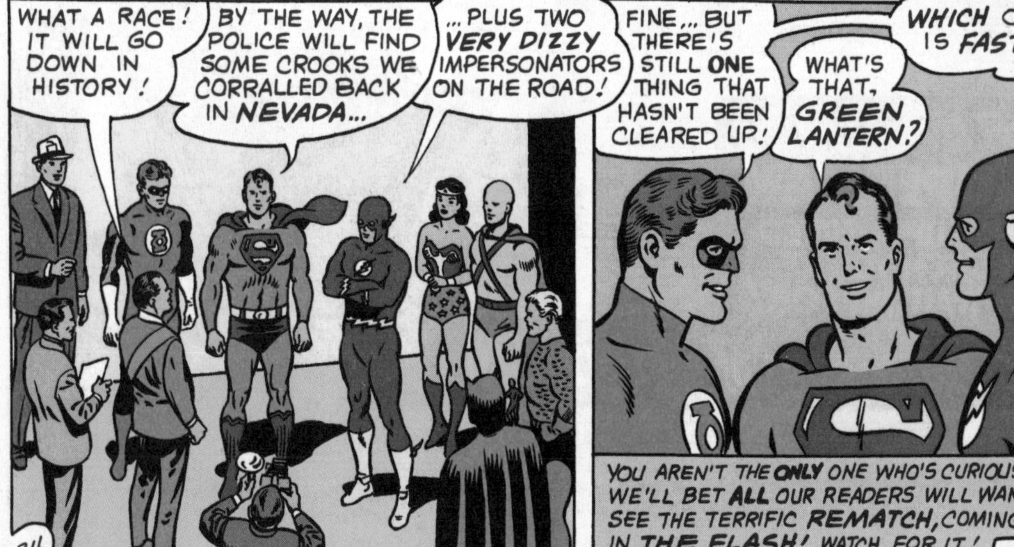
WHAT A RACE! IT WILL GO DOWN IN HISTORY!
BY THE WAY, THE POLICE WILL FIND SOME CROOKS WE CORRALLED BACK IN **NEVADA...**
...PLUS TWO **VERY DIZZY** IMPERSONATORS ON THE ROAD!
24
FINE,.. BUT THERE'S STILL **ONE** THING THAT HASN'T BEEN CLEARED UP!
WHAT'S THAT, **GREEN LANTERN?**
WHICH OF YOU IS **FASTER?**
YOU AREN'T THE **ONLY** ONE WHO'S CURIOUS, **G.L.!** WE'LL BET **ALL** OUR READERS WILL WANT TO SEE THE TERRIFIC **REMATCH,** COMING SOON IN **THE FLASH!** WATCH FOR IT!
THE END

SUPERMAN NATIONAL COMICS
DC
The FLASH
APPROVED BY THE COMICS CODE AUTHORITY
12¢
DEC. NO. 175
SUPERMAN-- I QUIT... I CAN'T... BEAT YOU...
I FINALLY GOT YOU TO ADMIT YOU'RE NOT THE FASTEST MAN ALIVE, FLASH!
FLASH Vs. SUPERMAN
IN THE SUPER-SPEED REMATCH YOU'VE BEEN WAITING FOR!
RACE to the END of the UNIVERSE!

STORY BY E. NELSON BRIDWELL

The FLASH

ART BY ROSS ANDRU and MIKE ESPOSITO

THE FLASH AND SUPERMAN ARE RACING... NOT ONLY TO SETTLE WHO IS THE FASTER, BUT TO SAVE THE LIFE OF A CITY! IF FLASH LOSES, CENTRAL CITY DIES; IF SUPERMAN FAILS, METROPOLIS PERISHES! SO WHY SHOULD THE MAN OF STEEL BE AIDING HIS FLASHY FOE?

I COULD ZOOM AHEAD OF FLASH NOW... BUT I MUST RESCUE HIM INSTEAD... EVEN IF IT MEANS MY FALLING FURTHER BEHIND!
ZZAT
ZZAT!

AND WHY SHOULD THE SCARLET SPEEDSTER TRY TO RESCUE THE METROPOLIS MARVEL... WHEN THE LIVES OF THOSE NEAREST AND DEAREST TO HIM... INCLUDING HIS WIFE, IRIS... DEPEND ON HIS WINNING?

SUPERMAN WILL PROBABLY BEAT ME IF I STOP TO SAVE HIM FROM THAT SPACE-VORTEX...
BUT I'LL HAVE TO TAKE THAT RISK!

THERE'S A COSMOS FULL OF CONUNDRUMS TO CRACK IN...

The RACE to the END of the UNIVERSE!

ONE EVENING, AN ANONYMOUS CALL COMES TO POLICE HEADQUARTERS IN CENTRAL CITY...
GET THIS... THE WEATHER WIZARD IS GONNA KNOCK OUT THE CITY POWER PLANT WITH LIGHTNIN' BOLTS! THEN HIS GANG WILL USE THE BLACKOUT TO COVER ITS LOOTIN'!
WAIT! WHO ARE YOU?
JUST SOMEONE WHO DOESN'T LIKE COSTUMED KOOKS MUSCLIN' IN ON HIS TERRITORY! CLICK!

MOMENTS LATER, A BULLETIN IS PICKED UP BY POLICE SCIENTIST BARRY ALLEN...
IT'S GETTING LATE BUT MY JOB IS FINISHED! I'LL RETURN THE LABMOBILE TO THE GARAGE AND...
ATTENTION, ALL CARS! A TIPSTER REPORTED THE WEATHER WIZARD IS PLANNING TO SABOTAGE CENTRAL CITY'S POWER PLANT WITH LIGHTNING BOLTS! PROCEED TO...
CENTRAL CITY POLICE DEPT.

THE WEATHER WIZARD, EH? EVER SINCE HE BROKE PRISON, I'VE BEEN WORKING ON THIS IMPROVED LIGHTNING ROD TO NEUTRALIZE THOSE BOLTS HE HURLS!
HERE'S MY CHANCE TO SEE HOW EFFECTIVE IT IS! BUT SINCE IT'D TAKE TOO LONG TO GET THERE IN THE LABMOBILE...

WITHDRAWING A RING FROM HIS POCKET, BARRY SLIPS IT ONTO HIS FINGER...
AND PRESSES A DEVICE THAT EJECTS A UNIFORM THAT RAPIDLY EXPANDS UPON CONTACT WITH AIR...

...AND A NANO-SECOND LATER, THE FANTABULOUS FIGURE OF THE FASTEST MAN ALIVE CAREENS THROUGH THE GATHERING DUSK...
I'LL SCOOT OVER THERE AS... THE FLASH!

BUT AS HE NEARS THE POWER PLANT...
STAND BY FOR ACTION, MEN!
TOO LATE! HE'S ALREADY SHOOTING BOLTS FROM HIS WEATHER WAND!
ZZAAT!!
ADMISSIONS
2

THIS CALLS FOR ULTRA-SPEED! I'LL HAVE TO GET THERE AND INSTALL THIS ROD...
...BEFORE THE LIGHTNING STRIKES!

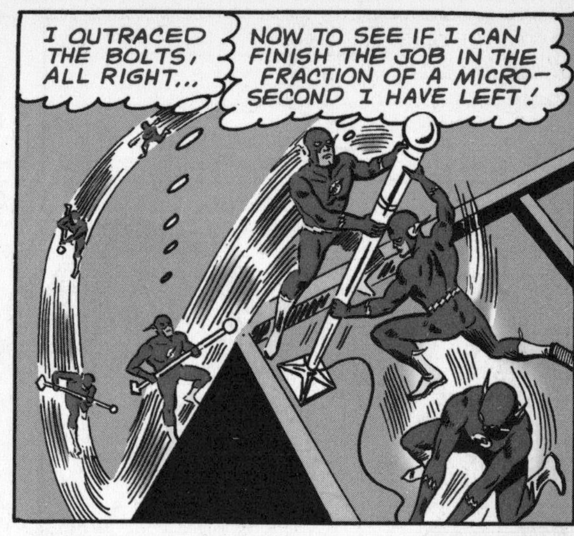
I OUTRACED THE BOLTS, ALL RIGHT...
NOW TO SEE IF I CAN FINISH THE JOB IN THE FRACTION OF A MICRO-SECOND I HAVE LEFT!

DID IT BEFORE THE BOLTS REACHED HERE--
EH?! WHERE ARE THE BOLTS? BY THIS TIME THEY SHOULD HAVE--

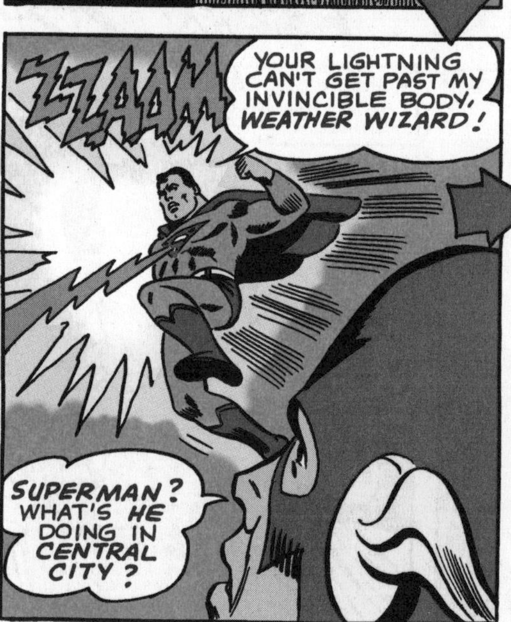
ZZAAM
YOUR LIGHTNING CAN'T GET PAST MY INVINCIBLE BODY, WEATHER WIZARD!
SUPERMAN? WHAT'S HE DOING IN CENTRAL CITY?

THEN, AS THE TWO COSTUMED CRIME-BUSTERS JOIN FORCES...
I DON'T THINK THE POWER COMPANY WILL MIND MY BORROWING THIS CABLE TO GIFT-WRAP A PACKAGE FOR THE POLICE!
AS FAR AS I'M CONCERNED, WEATHER WIZARD-- I'M NOT LETTING YOUR LIGHTNING BOLTS STRIKE EVEN... ONCE!
BLAST YOU, FLASH! I'LL... UUUHHH!
3

AFTER THE GANG HAS BEEN TURNED OVER TO THE POLICE...
WHY THE GRANDSTAND PLAY? I WAS DOING OKAY ON MY OWN!
SURE...THAT'S WHY YOU CALLED ME ON YOUR JUSTICE LEAGUE SIGNAL DEVICE!
COME OFF IT! I NEVER TOUCHED THE SIGNALER!
WHA-A-AT?

ALL I KNOW IS THAT A CALL CAME FOR ME... AND IT WAS ON YOUR SPECIAL WAVELENGTH!
IF YOU DIDN'T MAKE IT, WHO DID?
I'D GIVE A WEEK'S SALARY TO FIND OUT!

LATER, BACK IN HIS BARRY ALLEN IDENTITY, FLASH DISCUSSES THE CASE WITH HIS WIFE, IRIS...
I JUST DON'T GET IT! SUPERMAN MIGHT HAVE SPOTTED THE WEATHER WIZARD WITH HIS TELESCOPIC VISION... BUT THEN WHY DID HE HAVE TO COVER HIMSELF WITH THAT STORY ABOUT MY CALLING HIM?
ALL I KNOW, BARRY...

...IS THAT SUPERMAN IS A GOOD FRIEND OF YOURS! SURELY THERE MUST BE SOME LOGICAL EXPLANATION?
SURE THERE IS-- BUT I'D HATE TO THINK IT'S BECAUSE--
HE WAS MAKING ANOTHER TRY AT PROVING HE'S FASTER THAN I AM!

THE NEXT DAY, IN METROPOLIS, REPORTER CLARK KENT IS ON A ROUTINE ASSIGNMENT WHEN...
I HOPE YOU GOT YOUR BURIAL INSURANCE PAID UP, "BIG ANGIE"...
NO...PLEASE... GIVE ME A CHANCE--!
MEMBERS OF THE SOUTHSIDE MOB... ABOUT TO "RUB OUT" A MEMBER OF A RIVAL GANG!
A JOB FOR SUPERMAN!

CONCEALED BETWEEN PARKED CARS--REPORTER SWITCHES TO CRUSADER...
GREAT MOONS OF KRYPTON! THEY'VE ALREADY FIRED!
POW-
POW-
4

ONLY ONE CHANCE TO SAVE HIM...
AND THAT'S TO OUTRACE THE BULLETS!
POW!

MADE IT! NOW WHEN THE BULLETS HIT-- IT'LL BE AGAINST MY INVULNERABLE BODY!

STRANGE...! THOSE SLUGS SHOULD BE BOUNCING OFF ME BY NOW! WHAT...?

SIZZLING SUNS! FLASH... SNATCHING THE BULLETS OUT OF MID-AIR AS EASILY AS PICKING FLOWERS!
PLIP!
PLIP!
PLIP!

THEN, WITH THE DEADLY PROJECTILES DISPOSED OF...
OW! IS THIS FLASH-GUY ONE MAN OR A WHOLE REGIMENT?
HOLD IT, "BIG ANGIE"! THE POLICE WANT TO TALK TO YOU... ABOUT THAT JEWELRY HEIST LAST MONTH!
CORPORATION
5

ONCE MORE THE SULTANS OF CELEBRITY TURN THEIR CAPTIVES OVER TO THE LAW... AND WITH THE SAME SEQUEL...
ALL RIGHT, WHY THE GRAND-STAND PLAY, FLASH? I WAS DOING OKAY ON MY OWN!
THEY'RE THE SAME ONES I USED ON YOU YESTERDAY!
HUH? WHERE HAVE I HEARD THOSE WORDS BEFORE?
AND I SUPPOSE YOU'LL ALSO DENY YOU CALLED ME WITH YOUR JLA SIGNALER?

YOU BET YOUR WINGED BOOTS I'LL DENY IT!
THIS WHOLE THING HAS BEEN A RERUN OF YESTERDAY... WITH OUR ROLES REVERSED!
HMM--IT'S EVIDENT NOW THAT SOMEHOW, SOMEONE IS CUTTING IN ON OUR JLA WAVELENGTH!

YOU'RE RIGHT, FLASH... PERHAPS SOME ARCH-FOE IS TRYING TO TURN US AGAINST EACH OTHER!

ANOTHER SIGNAL! THIS TIME AN ALL-OUT ONE FOR A FULL-MEMBERSHIP EMERGENCY MEETING!

MY SUPER-HEARING HAS PICKED IT UP, TOO! MAYBE WE'RE ABOUT TO FIND OUT WHO'S BEHIND THIS--AND WHY!

WITH BLINDING BURSTS OF SUPER-SPEED, THEY STREAK FOR THE SECRET SANCTUARY...

AND AS THEY ENTER THE MEETING ROOM...
WHAT'S UP? WHY THE CALL?
YOU MEAN IT WASN'T EITHER ONE OF YOU TWO?
IT SURE WASN'T! LOOKS LIKE OUR HUNCH WAS RIGHT! SOMEONE'S BEEN CUTTING IN ON OUR SIGNAL DEVICES!
A SHREWD GUESS, SUPERMAN! IT WAS US!
6

WELL, I'LL BE A KRYPTONIAN BABOOTCH!
ROKK AND SORBAN! RULERS OF THE GAMBLERS' PLANET, VENTURA!*
ONCE WE CHECKED OUT OUR CONTROL OF FLASH'S AND SUPERMAN'S SIGNAL DEVICES--
WE TRIGGERED OFF THE GENERAL EMERGENCY SIGNAL AND USED THEIR SPECIAL VIBRATORY RATES TO TRAIL YOU TO YOUR SECRET HEADQUARTERS!
*EDITOR'S NOTE: SUPERMAN AND BATMAN LAST MET ROKK AND SORBAN IN WORLD'S FINEST COMICS #150, JUNE, 1965.

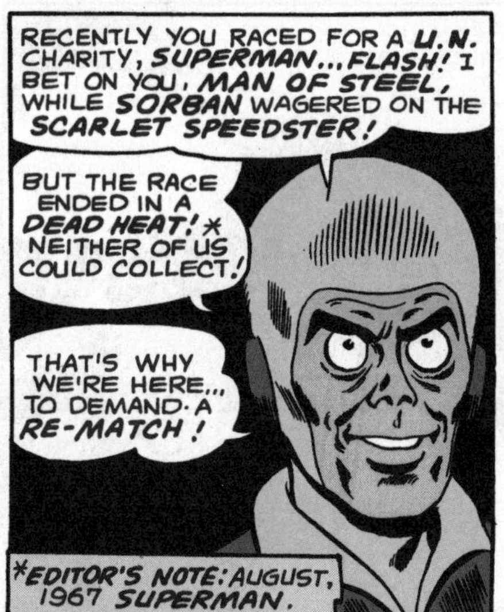
RECENTLY YOU RACED FOR A U.N. CHARITY, SUPERMAN...FLASH! I BET ON YOU, MAN OF STEEL, WHILE SORBAN WAGERED ON THE SCARLET SPEEDSTER!
BUT THE RACE ENDED IN A DEAD HEAT!* NEITHER OF US COULD COLLECT!
THAT'S WHY WE'RE HERE... TO DEMAND A RE-MATCH!
*EDITOR'S NOTE: AUGUST, 1967 SUPERMAN.

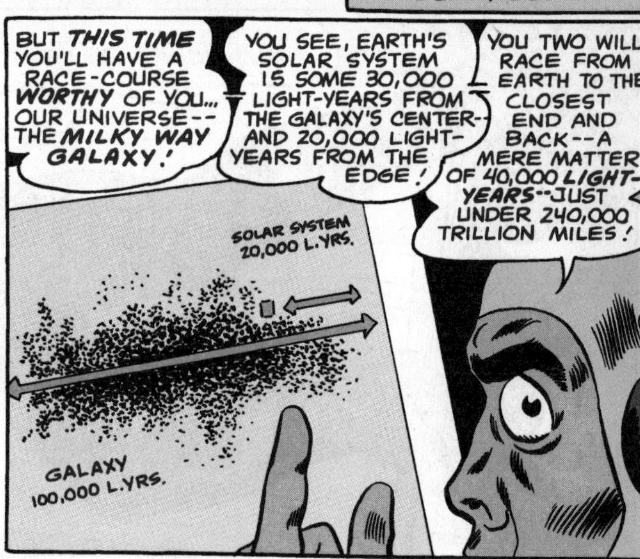
BUT THIS TIME YOU'LL HAVE A RACE-COURSE WORTHY OF YOU... OUR UNIVERSE--THE MILKY WAY GALAXY!
YOU SEE, EARTH'S SOLAR SYSTEM IS SOME 30,000 LIGHT-YEARS FROM THE GALAXY'S CENTER--AND 20,000 LIGHT-YEARS FROM THE EDGE!
YOU TWO WILL RACE FROM EARTH TO THE CLOSEST END AND BACK--A MERE MATTER OF 40,000 LIGHT-YEARS--JUST UNDER 240,000 TRILLION MILES!
SOLAR SYSTEM 20,000 L.YRS.
GALAXY 100,000 L.YRS.

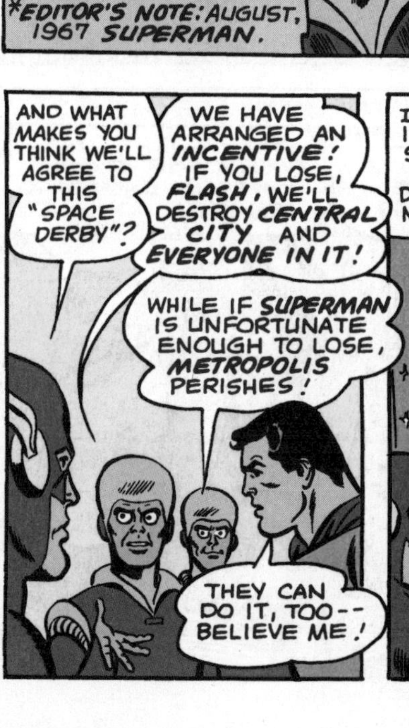
AND WHAT MAKES YOU THINK WE'LL AGREE TO THIS "SPACE DERBY"?
WE HAVE ARRANGED AN INCENTIVE! IF YOU LOSE, FLASH, WE'LL DESTROY CENTRAL CITY AND EVERYONE IN IT!
WHILE IF SUPERMAN IS UNFORTUNATE ENOUGH TO LOSE, METROPOLIS PERISHES!
THEY CAN DO IT, TOO--BELIEVE ME!

I'LL BELIEVE IT WHEN I SEE YOUR POWER DEMONSTRATED... NOT BEFORE!
FAIR ENOUGH! WATCH AS I ACTIVATE THAT MONITOR WITH MY MENTAL ENERGY!
COMING INTO VIEW IS THE PLANETOID EROS! IT IS DUE TO COLLIDE WITH EARTH IN THE YEAR 8819...
CLICK!

Y-YES--MY RAPID CALCULATIONS INDICATE YOU'RE RIGHT!
BUT NOW...I REMOVE THAT THREAT... BY DESTROYING EROS!
N-NOW...I... BELIEVE...
WHAM
7

SO IF WE REFUSE TO RACE IT OUT, YOU'LL DESTROY BOTH CITIES, EH?
PRECISELY!
BUT DON'T YOU REALIZE I CAN'T LIVE IN SPACE-- MUCH LESS RUN ACROSS IT, LIKE SUPERMAN?
THAT'S EASILY TAKEN CARE OF!

I'M CHARGING THE INVISIBLE AURA WHICH SURROUNDS YOUR BODY WITH SPECIAL ENERGY!
THERE IS NO PERFECT VACUUM IN SPACE! EVERYWHERE THERE IS MATTER, EVEN IF IT'S MERE COSMIC DUST... OR ATOMS!
PART OF THAT MATTER WILL BE AUTOMATICALLY TRANSMUTED TO OXYGEN TO KEEP YOU ALIVE, WHILE THE REST FORMS A RUNWAY FOR YOU!

THAT'S ENOUGH! LET'S BREAK UP THIS FARCE RIGHT NOW! THEY CAN'T HANDLE ALL OF US!
WHAT AN AMUSING SPECTACLE, ROKK!

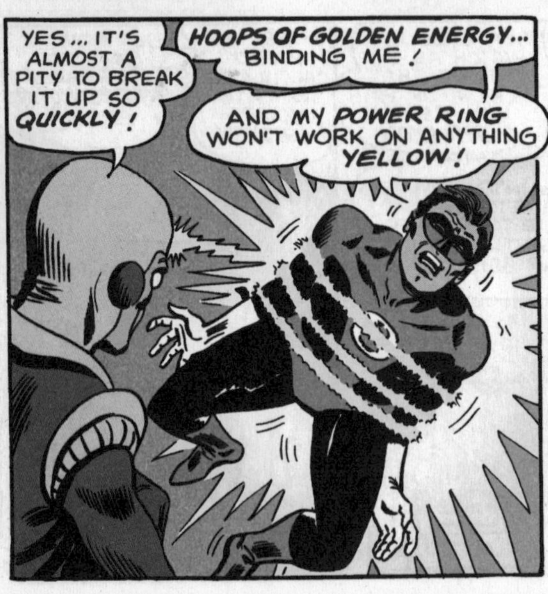
YES... IT'S ALMOST A PITY TO BREAK IT UP SO QUICKLY!
HOOPS OF GOLDEN ENERGY... BINDING ME!
AND MY POWER RING WON'T WORK ON ANYTHING YELLOW!

AS THE MARTIAN MANHUNTER CHARGES FORWARD...
GASP! FIRE... MY ONE WEAKNESS!
DON'T WORRY... THE FIRE CAGE IS ONLY POWERFUL ENOUGH TO WEAKEN YOU--NOT KILL YOU!
8

AS WONDER WOMAN REACHES FOR HER MAGIC LASSO...
SUFFERING SAPPHO! CAUGHT BY MY OWN LASSO!
AND WHILE I HOLD IT, YOU MUST OBEY ME! HA, HA!

A TRANSPARENT SHOWER STALL DESCENDS OVER AQUAMAN, AND...
THE SHOWER... WHICH KEEPS ME ALIVE BY SPRINKLING ME WITH WATER EVERY HOUR... HAS PARALYZED ME!

SIMULTANEOUSLY...BATMAN, GREEN ARROW, HAWKMAN AND ATOM, TOO, ARE RENDERED HELPLESS...
WE'RE ALL BOUND...CAN'T MOVE!
AND I'M... FROZEN... IN THIS POSITION!
CAN'T EVEN ACTIVATE THE... SIZE-AND-WEIGHT CONTROLS... IN MY GLOVES!

MOMENTS LATER, OUTSIDE THE SANCTUARY...
I SHOULD WARN YOU, FLASH, THAT YOUR OXYGEN WILL LAST ONLY ONE EARTHLY WEEK! YOU HAD BETTER FINISH THE RACE BY THEN!
YOUR HONORARY MEMBER, SNAPPER CARR, WILL FIRE THE STARTING PISTOL!
I'D LIKE TO USE IT AGAINST THEM -- B-BUT... I... C-CAN'T!
ON YOUR MARK... GET SET...

POW!
GO!
9

AS THE TWO ROCKET OFF INTO THE COSMOS, ONE THOUGHT HAUNTS THE FLASH ...
I MUST GO MANY TIMES FASTER THAN EVER BEFORE! IF I LOSE THIS RACE, ALL CENTRAL CITY WILL BE BLASTED INTO OBLIVION! IRIS... HER FATHER, PROF. WEST... MY FRIENDS, DEXTER MYLES AND AL DESMOND...

AND SIMILAR CONSIDERATIONS CROWD INTO SUPERMAN'S BRAIN...
I MUST WIN! OTHERWISE, METROPOLIS IS DOOMED... AND SO ARE MY FRIENDS... LOIS LANE, JIMMY OLSEN, PERRY WHITE, LANA LANG...

THE RACERS REMAIN NECK-AND-NECK FOR DOZENS OF LIGHT-YEARS, UNTIL...
AHEAD OF ME--A SOLAR SYSTEM WITH A RED SUN! I HAVE NO SUPER-POWERS UNDER SUCH A SUN... I'LL HAVE TO MAKE A DETOUR!
THIS IS A LUCKY BREAK FOR ME!

AT MULTI-LIGHT SPEED, THE MAN OF STEEL HURTLES TO A YELLOW SUN SYSTEM...
WHY... THIS IS THE SYSTEM WHERE VENTURA, ROKK AND SORBAN'S HOME WORLD, IS LOCATED!
I'LL TAKE A QUICK PEEK AT IT WITH MY TELESCOPIC VISION!

GREAT GALAXIES! A GIGANTIC VOLCANO ERUPTING ON VENTURA!
THOUSANDS MAY DIE UNLESS I RESCUE THEM!
10

HAS SUPERMAN ABANDONED THE VENTURANS TO THEIR FATE? WHAT DID HE SEE THAT MADE HIM SUDDENLY DECIDE TO ABANDON THE RACE? STORY CONTINUES ON THE FOLLOWING PAGE!

MEANWHILE, WHAT HAS BEEN HAPPENING TO THE SUPER-SPEEDING FLASH?
STRANGE... THAT LOOKS LIKE A DERELICT SPACE-SHIP!
IT CAN'T BE FROM EARTH, THOUGH! OUR ASTRONAUTS HAVEN'T EVEN REACHED THE MOON YET!
AND THERE ARE FIGURES INSIDE... LIKE MEN IN SPACE-SUITS!

OBVIOUSLY, THIS SHIP IS DAMAGED! I BETTER TAKE TIME OUT TO SEE IF I CAN HELP THE MEN INSIDE!

WHY, THESE AREN'T MEN AT ALL! THEY'RE SOME SORT OF PULPY GROWTH ATTACHED TO THE INSIDE OF THE SHIP'S HULL!
KRAMM
EH? THAT OUTER DOOR ISN'T DAMAGED! IT CLOSED BEHIND ME!

UHH! CAN'T BREATHE! SOMEHOW, MY OXYGEN-PRODUCING AURA HAS STOPPED WORKING!
GASP! I FEEL WEAK...TOO WEAK TO VIBRATE THROUGH THE HULL! I'M TRAPPED!

...AND BACK AT THE JLA SANCTUARY ON EARTH...
HA, HA! FLASH IS FINISHED! HE'LL NEVER ESCAPE FROM THAT TRAP!
12

BUT SUDDENLY...
OXYGEN... POURING IN AROUND ME... REVIVING ME!
WHAT'S GOING ON HERE?

AT LEAST I'VE GOT MY SPEED BACK... CAN VIBRATE OUT OF HERE... PASSING THE MOLECULES OF MY BODY BETWEEN THOSE OF THE SHIP!

OUTSIDE... A STUNNING REVELATION...
GREAT STARS! THE SHIP HAS CHANGED ITS SHAPE! I'M BEGINNING TO CATCH ON--
THE "SPACESHIP" IS REALLY A PLANT! IT ASSUMED THAT SHAPE IN ORDER TO LURE OXYGEN-BREATHING BEINGS TO IT! LIKE ALL PLANTS, IT "BREATHES" CARBON DIOXIDE WHICH ANIMALS EXHALE, AND GIVES OFF OXYGEN!
IT TEMPORARILY CUT OFF MY OXYGEN WHILE IT TOOK IN THE CARBON DIOXIDE I BREATHED OUT... THEN AUTO-MATICALLY REVIVED ME WHEN IT EXHALED "WASTE"!

NOW WHAT'S THE REACTION OF THE ALIEN GAMBLERS BACK ON EARTH?
BAH! FLASH HELD OUT LONGER THAN I THOUGHT HE COULD! HE'S ESCAPED--
FOR A WHILE! THE NEXT TRAP IS BOUND TO GET HIM!

THIS SMELLS FISHIER THAN A SARDINE CANNERY! SORBAN IS SUPPOSED TO BE BETTING ON FLASH ... SO WHY DOES HE WANT HIM TO FALL INTO A DOOM-TRAP?
13

SOON, THE METROPOLIS MARVEL CATCHES UP WITH THE CRIMSON COMET IN ANOTHER SOLAR SYSTEM...
I'VE TRIED MY SIGNAL DEVICE... BUT THOSE VILLAINS HAVE FOULED IT UP! THEY PROBABLY DID THE SAME TO THE OTHERS, TOO! SINCE I CAN'T SPEAK IN SPACE, I MUST "TALK" TO FLASH WITH MY HANDS!
FLASH... DANGER... URGENT WE TURN BACK!

NO... I'M NOT FALLING FOR YOUR TRICK!
THAT'S A SURPRISE! SUPERMAN MUST BE DESPERATE TO TRY TO GET ME TO QUIT THE RACE!

JUST THEN, ANOTHER OBSTACLE ON THE RACE-COURSE LOOMS BEFORE THEM...
KRYPTONITE METEORS! THAT'S THE ONE SUBSTANCE THAT CAN KILL ME! I'LL HAVE TO DETOUR... AGAIN!
ANOTHER BREAK FOR ME!

MY TELESCOPIC VISION SHOWED FLASH WAS ENDANGERED THE LAST TIME I PARTED FROM HIM...
I'D BETTER KEEP AN EVEN CLOSER WATCH ON HIM THIS TIME!

AS THE FIGURE OF THE MAN OF MIGHT VANISHES FROM THE MONITOR SCREEN...
GOOD! FLASH IS RUNNING ACROSS THE METEORS, WHICH HAVE FORMED A PATH FOR HIM!
EVERTHING'S GOING PERFECTLY! AND WITH SUPERMAN OUT OF THE WAY...
WHO SAYS I AM?

SUPERMAN! IMPOSSIBLE! EVEN YOU COULDN'T HAVE COME BACK HERE THAT FAST!
DON'T WORRY... I BROUGHT ALONG SOMETHING FOR JUST SUCH AN EMERGENCY...
14

...GOLD KRYPTONITE!
GREEN KRYPTONITE CAN KILL YOU, SUPERMAN! BUT THIS GOLD K'S GOOD ENOUGH TO PERMANENTLY REMOVE YOUR POWERS!

GREAT GUARDIANS! SUPERMAN'S LOST HIS POWERS! HE'S COLLAPSING--!
NOT EVEN MY POWER RING COULD HELP HIM... IT DOESN'T WORK ON ANYTHING YELLOW!

LOOK! SUPERMAN'S CHANGING!
INCREDIBLE! HE'S...

...THE MARTIAN MANHUNTER!

YES... YOUR FLAME CAGE WASN'T QUITE STRONG ENOUGH TO KEEP ME FROM USING MY SHAPE-CHANGING POWER! WHEN I BECAME "SUPERMAN" I GAINED HIS IMMUNITY TO FIRE!
BUT I HAD HIS WEAKNESS, TOO! THE GOLD K REMOVED MY POWER TO DUPLICATE SUPERMAN AGAIN... BUT AT LEAST YOU WON'T USE IT ON HIM! MY MARTIAN SCIENCE HAS TURNED IT TO LEAD!

VERY CLEVER, MANHUNTER! I SEE I'D BETTER INCREASE THE FIRE'S POWER TO KEEP YOU FROM USING YOUR SHAPE-SHIFTING SKILL AGAIN!
15

WITH THAT SIDE-PLAY OUT OF THE WAY, LET'S GET BACK TO THE FLASH...
I'M NEARLY AT THE END OF MY METEOR PATH! HMM... THIS LAST ONE ISN'T KRYPTONITE!

BUT AS THE SULTAN OF SPEED SETS FOOT ON THE METEOROID...
UHHH! THIS ONE ISN'T SOLID!
IT'S SOFT AND STICKY!

CAN'T VIBRATE THROUGH THIS STUFF! I'M ONLY GETTING MYSELF MORE STUCK UP... LIKE BRER RABBIT WITH THE TAR BABY!

A QUICK SHIFT BACK TO THE MEETING ROOM...
IF ONLY I COULD SEND FLASH HELP WITH MY POWER RING!
BUT THAT'S OUT! IT'S BEEN MORE THAN 24 HOURS SINCE I RECHARGED MY RING -- AND IT'S RUN OUT OF POWER!

CHEER UP, GL! OTHER HELPFUL EYES HAVE BEEN KEEPING TABS ON THE SCARLET SPEEDSTER...
I ANTICIPATED FLASH WOULD GET IN DANGER AS SOON AS WE PARTED COMPANY!
THIS ORDINARY METEOR I PLUCKED OUT OF SPACE SHOULD HELP HIM OUT!

BULL'S-EYE!
KLUNK
THE IMPACT'S KNOCKING HIM TOWARD A NEARBY PLANET WITH AN EARTH-LIKE ATMOSPHERE!
16

SUPERMAN'S STRATEGY IS REVEALED AS THE "QUICK-SAND" METEOR SPEEDS THROUGH THE PLANET'S ATMOSPHERE...
I DON'T KNOW HOW THIS HAPPENED, BUT NOW THAT WE'RE HURTLING THROUGH OXYGEN-AIR, THE FRICTION IS BURNING THE METEOR!
AND MY AURA PROTECTS ME FROM FRICTION-INDUCED HEAT!

HAVE TO GET BACK INTO THE RACE! BY WHIRLING, I CAN SET UP A TORNADO OF AIR WHICH'LL LIFT ME BACK INTO SPACE!
ALL THAT'S LEFT OF THE BIG METEOR ARE TWO FRAGMENTS OF GREEN K THAT WERE EMBEDDED IN IT!

IN THAT ATMOSPHERE, I CAN SPEAK TO FLASH..., WARN HIM...
OH, NO! GREEN K... WEAKENING ME!
BUT I CAN STILL WARN HIM... WITH SUPER-VENTRILOQUISM! *

*EDITOR'S NOTE: ALTHOUGH ORDINARY VENTRILOQUISTS ONLY CREATE AN ILLUSION OF THROWING THEIR VOICES, SUPERMAN CAN ACTUALLY DO IT THROUGH SUPER-VENTRILOQUISM!

FLASH! THIS IS ALL A TRAP... FOR YOU! TURN BACK TO EARTH... PLEASE!
NOT ON YOUR LIFE, PAL! SOUNDS LIKE YOU JUST WANT ME TO GIVE UP, SO YOU CAN SAVE METROPOLIS!
17

THE GREEN K PASSES... THE MAN OF STEEL RECOVERS... AND THE RACE CONTINUES...
I'M GOING CLEAR THROUGH THIS YELLOW SUN! I'LL WRAP YOU IN MY INDESTRUCTIBLE CAPE AND TAKE YOU THROUGH! *
NOTHING DOING! IT'S NOT THAT I DON'T TRUST YOU... BUT WHY TAKE CHANCES? I'LL DETOUR THIS TIME!

*EDITOR'S NOTE: FLASH IS ONLY IMMUNE TO FRICTION-HEAT, NOT TO THE SEARING FLAMES OF THE SUN.

BUT AS FLASH PASSES ONE OF THE YELLOW STAR'S PLANETS--SPACESHIPS HURTLE UP AT HIM AND...
AN INTRUDER! DESTROY HIM!
WE HAVE HAD ENOUGH TROUBLE WITH ALIEN INVADERS IN THE PAST! THIS WILL SERVE NOTICE THAT OUR WORLD IS OFF LIMITS!
ZZAT
THOSE WEIRD VIBRATORY RAYS... ADJUSTING TO MY OWN VIBRATIONS! THE ONLY WAY TO AVOID DEATH-- IS BY DODGING THEM ALL!

HOWEVER, BEHIND A NEARBY ASTEROID IS SUPERMAN!
LUCKY FOR THE STUBBORN FLASH I'M KEEPING TABS ON HIM!
LOOKS LIKE I'LL HAVE TO GET HIM OUT OF ANOTHER SCRAPE!
ZZAT! ZZAT-

TWIN BEAMS OF HEAT-VISION SPEAR THROUGH THE VOID, AND...
THOSE GUNS MELTING! DOES IT MEAN...?
SSSS
SSSSS

SHORTLY, AS THE HUMAN THUNDERBOLT HURTLES ON...
SURE ENOUGH... SUPERMAN'S BEHIND ME! YET I HAD TO DETOUR!
WHY SHOULD HE HELP ME?

THE TWO COMPETITORS RACE ON, FROM SUN TO SUN... REACH THE END OF THE GALAXY... AND ARE ON THEIR WAY BACK, WHEN...
TIRED... SO TERRIBLY TIRED... I MUST REST!
BUT SUPERMAN NEVER TIRES! HE MUST HAVE REALIZED THAT GAVE HIM THE ADVANTAGE! THAT'S WHY HE AIDED ME!
18

THIS PLANET... I'LL LAND HERE!
SPINNING SATELLITES! WHAT'S FLASH UP TO NOW?
I'LL TAG ALONG!

AS FLASH LANDS ON THE ALIEN WORLD'S SURFACE, FOLLOWED BY SUPERMAN...
ALL RIGHT--YOU WIN, SUPERMAN! I'M TOO TIRED TO FINISH THE RACE!
QUITTING, EH? ADMITTING AT LAST YOU'RE NOT THE FASTEST MAN ALIVE!

AS THE DEJECTED SPEEDSTER SITS ALONE...
I'VE FAILED... FAILED IRIS... MY FRIENDS... ALL OF CENTRAL CITY!
FLASH-- FLASH--

WHAT? HOW COULD ANYONE HERE KNOW MY NAME?
I KNOW IT! LISTEN TO ME!
IMPOSSIBLE! I CAN'T BELIEVE IT!

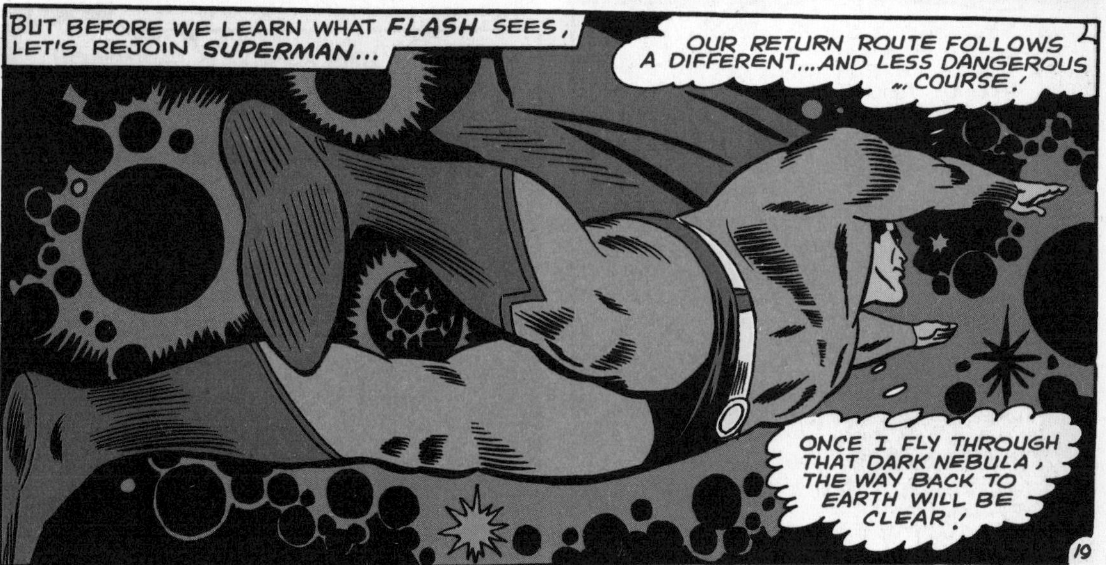
BUT BEFORE WE LEARN WHAT FLASH SEES, LET'S REJOIN SUPERMAN...
OUR RETURN ROUTE FOLLOWS A DIFFERENT...AND LESS DANGEROUS ...COURSE!
ONCE I FLY THROUGH THAT DARK NEBULA, THE WAY BACK TO EARTH WILL BE CLEAR!
19

WITHOUT WARNING...
A VORTEX HAS SUDDENLY WHIPPED UP INSIDE THIS NEBULA! IT'S BATTERING ME--DRAWING ME TOWARD ITS CENTER!
BY THE MOONS OF KRYPTON! AT THE EYE OF THE VORTEX... THE ENTRANCE TO ANOTHER DIMENSION!

UHHH! NO USE! NOT EVEN I CAN WITHSTAND THIS "SPACE HURRICANE"! I NEED HELP!
BUT WHO? FLASH IS THE ONLY ONE NEAR ENOUGH TO GET HERE IN TIME...AND HE'S BUSHED!

STILL, HE'S MY ONLY HOPE! I'LL BEAM HIM A MESSAGE WITH MY HEAT VISION!

AND ON THE PLANET WHERE FLASH SITS...
THAT MESSAGE I JUST RECEIVED--WHAT AN INCREDIBLE REVELATION... THE TRUTH ABOUT THIS RACE!
WAIT... ANOTHER MESSAGE BEING CARVED ON THAT STONE... BY HEAT BEAMS!
FLASH
NEED HELP
URGENT
SUPERMA

WITH SPEED THAT WOULD SHAME THE SWIFTEST ROCKET, THE CRIMSON COMET STREAKS UP FROM THE PLANET...
TO THINK I WAS READY TO QUIT! WELL, TIRED OR NOT, I'M GOING ON!
HANG ON, SUPERMAN! HERE I COME!
20

REACHING THE EERIE VORTEX, THE MONARCH OF MOTION JOINS THE MONARCH OF MIGHT IN HIS TITANIC TUSSLE...
IT'S WORKING! BY RACING TOGETHER IN THE DIRECTION OPPOSITE TO THE VORTEX'S SPIN, WE'RE COUNTERING IT... DESTROYING IT!
WHAT A PAL! FLASH CAME THROUGH, AFTER ALL!

OKAY... NOW LET'S FINISH THIS RACE!
THERE'S MORE THAN A VICTORY IN THIS CONTEST AT STAKE NOW!

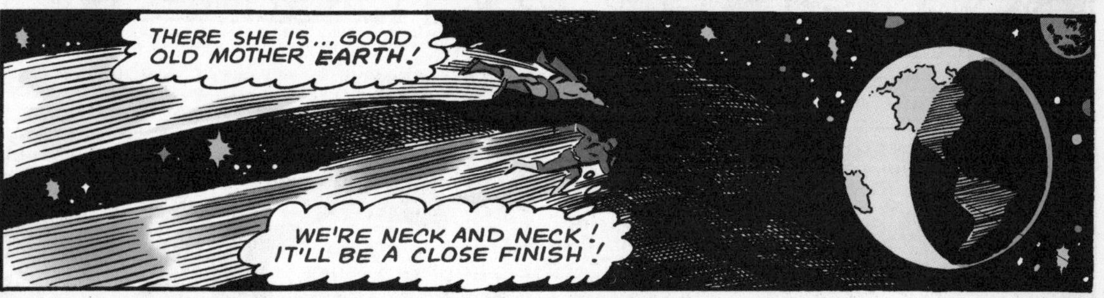
THERE SHE IS... GOOD OLD MOTHER EARTH!
WE'RE NECK AND NECK! IT'LL BE A CLOSE FINISH!

A SPLIT-SECOND LATER, IN THE SANCTUARY...
SUPERMAN WINS! HE CROSSED THE FINISH LINE FIRST!
FINISH

IT'S OVER! THE 3-D MONITOR SHOWS FLASH WON!
FINISH

AN INSTANT LATER, THE MAN OF STEEL ENTERS AND CONFRONTS ROKK...
STAY BACK, SUPERMAN, OR I'LL DESTROY YOU WITH THIS HORDE OF MAGICAL DEMONS I'VE CONJURED UP!
THAT'S THE FIRST TIME ROKK EVER CLAIMED MAGICAL POWERS!
21

...BUT, THEN, YOU AREN'T REALLY ROKK, ARE YOU?

SINCE THOSE SPACE-TRAPS DIDN'T FINISH YOU, FLASH-- IT LOOKS LIKE I'LL HAVE TO DO IT--PERSONALLY!

YOU'RE MIGHTY FAST FOR A VENTURAN, SORBAN!

YOU FORGET, THOUGH, THAT I'VE BEEN RUNNING FASTER THAN YOU'VE EVER DREAMED OF GOING IN THE PAST WEEK!
NOW I CAN RUN RINGS AROUND YOU... PROFESSOR ZOOM!

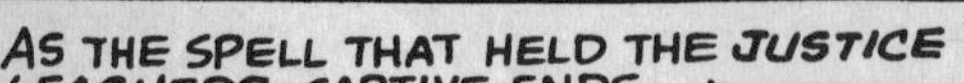

AS THE SPELL THAT HELD THE JUSTICE LEAGUERS CAPTIVE ENDS...

AND "ROKK" IS REALLY ABRA KADABRA, THE MAGICIAN FROM THE 64TH CENTURY! HIS "MAGIC" COULDN'T HURT ME BECAUSE IT'S REALLY FUTURISTIC SCIENCE!

WH-WHAT DID YOU CALL HIM, FLASH?
PROFESSOR ZOOM... OTHERWISE KNOWN AS THE REVERSE-FLASH FROM THE 25TH CENTURY! ONLY HE COULD HAVE HAD SUCH SPEED!
THAT BLOW-UP OF EROS WAS ONLY AN ILLUSION HE CREATED!

"I LEARNED THEY WERE IMPOSTORS WHEN I SPOTTED THE REAL ROKK AND SORBAN ON VENTURA...GAMBLING AS USUAL!"

IF ROKK AND SORBAN ARE HERE... WHO'S IN THE SANCTUARY?

MY VOLCANO ERUPTED FIRST, ROKK! I WIN!

TELL ME, GREEN LANTERN.. HOW DID YOU MANAGE TO GET THAT MESSAGE TO ME?

I HAVE A RESERVE POWER LEFT IN MY RING AFTER MY 24 HOURS ARE UP... TO PROTECT ME! NORMALLY, I CAN'T USE IT... BUT BY EXERTING ALL MY WILL POWER, I SOMETIMES CAN! *

THIS TIME I EXPANDED, TEMPORARILY, AQUAMAN'S ABILITY TO COMMUNICATE TELEPATHICALLY WITH SEA CREATURES!

*EDITOR'S NOTE: GL DID THIS TO SAVE HIS FRIEND PIEFACE, IN GREEN LANTERN #46, "DEATH OF A GLADIATOR!"

"THAT EXPLAINS WHY I GOT YOUR MESSAGE FROM A FISH THAT COULD IMITATE HUMAN SPEECH!"

I HAVE A MESSAGE FROM GREEN LANTERN-AQUAMAN...THE RACE IS A FAKE...TO LEAD YOU INTO DEADLY TRAPS!

22

OUR PLAN TO DESTROY OUR FOE FAILED...YET YOU COULD HAVE KILLED FLASH BEFORE HE GOT BACK, KADABRA! WHY DIDN'T YOU JUST CUT OFF HIS OXYGEN SUPPLY WITH YOUR MAGIC?
BUT I DID! I STILL DON'T KNOW HOW HE SURVIVED!
I ARRANGED IT! I INHALED A LUNGFUL OF RESERVE OXYGEN ON VENTURA IN CASE YOU PULLED THAT STUNT! THEN I EXHALED IT OUT ON FLASH WHEN YOU DID JUST THAT!

ONE THING, THOUGH..., I DIDN'T NOTICE WHICH OF US WON!
NEITHER DID I!

IT WAS FLASH!
NO... SUPERMAN!
WILD! THE FINISH MUST HAVE LOOKED DIFFERENT FROM DIFFERENT ANGLES!
HOW ABOUT IT, READERS? WHICH OF US DO YOU THINK WON?
LOOK AT THE PICTURES OF THE FINISH ON PAGE 21 AND MAKE UP YOUR OWN MIND!
THE END
23

SUPERMAN
VS
The
FLASH

WORLD'S FINEST
COMICS
DC WORLD'S FINEST
PRESENTS
SUPERMAN and THE FLASH
APPROVED BY THE COMICS CODE AUTHORITY
NOV.
NO. 198
15¢
THEY'RE OFF!
THE THIRD RACE BETWEEN THE WORLD'S FASTEST SUPER-HEROES! AND THIS TIME THERE MUST BE A WINNER!

ALWAYS, THERE ARE THE QUESTIONS WHICH SEEM TO BE UNANSWERABLE! THE GALAXY-SPANNING ADVENTURE YOU ARE ABOUT TO WITNESS WILL ANSWER AT LEAST ONE--!
IT BEGINS THIS AUTUMN MORNING IN THE APARTMENT OF REPORTER JIMMY OLSEN--
OBOYOBOY... MY HEAD FEELS LIKE THE INSIDE OF A VOLCANO! I WAS UP ALL NIGHT COVERING THAT POLITICAL CONVENTION--
--AND THOSE SMOKE-FILLED ROOMS ARE MURDER!
S-508

GOT TO LOAD UP ON ASPIRIN... AND TAKE A COLD SHOWER--

SUDDENLY, THE FLOOR SEEMS TO MELT FROM UNDER JIMMY'S BARE FEET... HE IS FALLING, FALLING, FALLING...

-- AND, *INCREDIBLY,* COMES TO REST IN A *ROMAN CHARIOT,* TEARING AROUND A DUSTY RACE TRACK... NEARLY *TWO THOUSAND* YEARS AGO--!

PRESENTING
SUPERMAN
AND
The FLASH

AND, AS JIMMY FALLS THROUGH A GAP IN TIME, SO DOES ONE *MAXIMUS FLAVIUS*-- OCCUPATION: ROMAN SOLDIER!
2

IN A MIND-STAGGERING
"RACE TO SAVE THE UNIVERSE!"

STORY BY: DENNY O'NEIL, ART BY: DICK DILLIN & JOE GIELLA, EDITING BY: JULIUS SCHWARTZ

SOME SORT OF DISTURBANCE DOWN IN THE STREET!
GOOD--! THIS PATROL WAS GETTING DULL!
3

HEY, WHATSA BIG IDEA, BUDDY-BOY? --I MEAN, I AIN'T HACKIN' UP YER CHARIOT, AM I?
SURROUNDED BY SMOKE-BELCHING, ILL-SMELLING DRAGONS! WHAT MANNER OF EVIL WIZARDRY HAS FORE-PASSED?
POOR GUY-- PROBABLY THINKS HE'S CAESAR AT THE RUBICON!

HERE IS THE FIENDISH MAGICIAN! I'LL FEED HIM MY SWORD-EDGE!
OKAY, FELLA... GET IT OUT OF YOUR SYSTEM! TRY TO HACK ME!

I COULD'VE TOLD YOU IT WAS A WASTE OF GOOD STEEL! BUT YOUR KIND ALWAYS HAS TO LEARN THE HARD WAY!
WOE HAS INDEED BEFALLEN ME!

I WON'T BOTHER TRYING TO QUESTION YOU--! YOU NEED HELP-- MEDICAL HELP!
THE BARBARIAN SORCERER BABBLES! I CANNOT UNDERSTAND HIS SPEECH!
ATTENTION, SUPERMAN OF EARTH!

ONE OF THE GUARDIANS -- GREEN LANTERN'S BOSSES! BUT... WHY IS HE CONTACTING ME?-- INSTEAD OF GL?
HEED MY TELEPATHIC REQUEST, TERRAN! REPORT TO OA, IMMEDIATELY!
4

THAT SOUNDED URGENT! COME ON, FELLA... YOU'RE GOING WITH ME ON A TRIP!
WE'LL TAKE A SHORT CUT THROUGH THIS SPACE-WARP!
SURELY I HAVE PASSED BEYOND THE MORTAL REALM!

MORE QUICKLY THAN YOU CAN READ THESE WORDS, THE CAPED KRYPTONIAN TRANSVERSES THE YAWNING EMPTINESS THAT MARGINS THE STARS...AND ARRIVES AT A TINY WORLD HOVERING NEAR THE EDGE OF THE GALAXY--

--OA, HOME OF THE IMMORTAL GUARDIANS...
WELCOME TO OUR SOIL, VENERABLE JUSTICE-FIGHTER!
THANKS...THOUGH I CAN'T GUESS WHY YOU CALLED! WHAT PROBLEM COULD YOU POSSIBLY HAVE THAT YOUR CORPS OF LANTERNS COULDN'T HANDLE?
HAVE I PASSED UNTO OLYMPUS, OR--?

A VERY GRAVE PROBLEM, INDEED--ONE WHICH THREATENS THE ENTIRE UNIVERSE!
OUR SENSOR-TACHYON-INDICATOR SHOWS US THAT THE ANACHRONIDS HAVE PASSED INTO OUR SPACE!

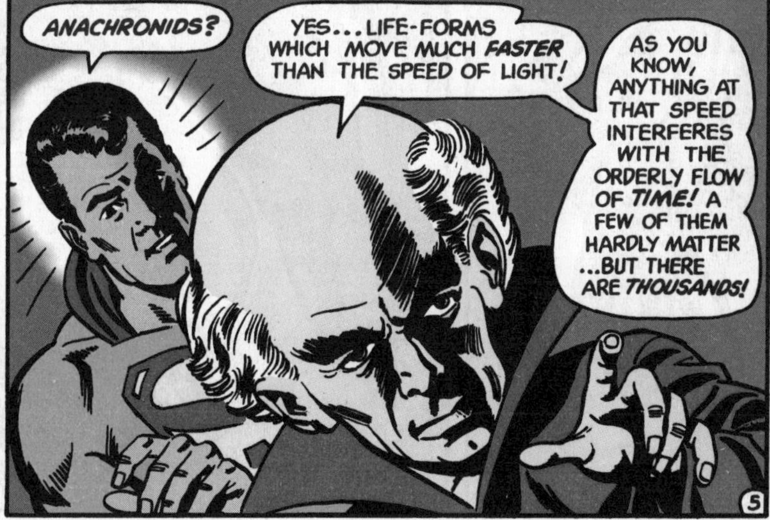
ANACHRONIDS?
YES...LIFE-FORMS WHICH MOVE MUCH FASTER THAN THE SPEED OF LIGHT!
AS YOU KNOW, ANYTHING AT THAT SPEED INTERFERES WITH THE ORDERLY FLOW OF TIME! A FEW OF THEM HARDLY MATTER ...BUT THERE ARE THOUSANDS!
5

THIS MEANS THAT UNLESS STEPS ARE TAKEN, THE VERY FABRIC OF TIME WILL SUNDER--

...THE PAST WILL MELT INTO THE PRESENT... DESTROYING BOTH!
THAT EXPLAINS THIS MAN... HE'S REALLY A ROMAN CENTURION! IT'S ALREADY BEGUN!
WHAT CAN I-- OR ANYONE-- DO?

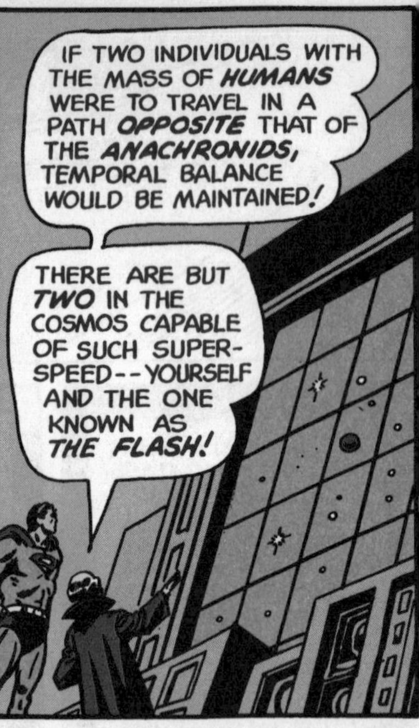
IF TWO INDIVIDUALS WITH THE MASS OF HUMANS WERE TO TRAVEL IN A PATH OPPOSITE THAT OF THE ANACHRONIDS, TEMPORAL BALANCE WOULD BE MAINTAINED!
THERE ARE BUT TWO IN THE COSMOS CAPABLE OF SUCH SUPER-SPEED--YOURSELF AND THE ONE KNOWN AS THE FLASH!

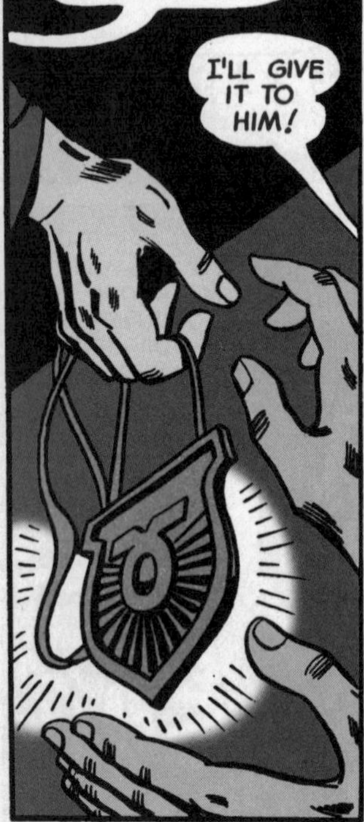
YOU HAVE UNLIMITED ENDURANCE AND IMMUNITY FROM HARM! THE FLASH, WE KNOW, DOES NOT--
--HOWEVER, LET HIM WEAR THIS MEDALLION! IT WILL PROTECT HIM EVEN AS THE RINGS PROTECT THE GREEN LANTERN CORPS!
I'LL GIVE IT TO HIM!

I'VE MEMORIZED THE PATH WE HAVE TO TAKE... WE'LL START IMMEDIATELY!
WE SHALL CARE FOR THE ROMAN... AND OBSERVE YOUR PROGRESS ON OUR VIEWERS! FAREWELL---AND GOOD FORTUNE!

I DID NOT TELL SUPERMAN THAT SUCH IS THE STRENGTH OF THE MEDALLION THAT IT DRAINS ALL THE POWER OF OUR POWER BATTERIES...
UNTIL THE FLASH HAS FINISHED HIS TASK, OUR CORPS WILL BE HELPLESS!---THE UNIVERSE COMPLETELY UNPROTECTED!
6

MOMENTS LATER, ON EARTH... THE MAN OF STEEL QUICKLY EXPLAINS THE SITUATION TO HIS FELLOW JUSTICE LEAGUER!...

...AND HERE'S THE GADGET THAT'LL KEEP YOU ALIVE IN SPACE! IT SHOULD ALSO KEEP YOU FROM BECOMING EXHAUSTED... AND PAVE A ROADWAY FOR YOU TO RUN ON...
--PROVIDED I DYE THE YELLOW SOLES OF MY BOOTS!*
I REALIZE THE GRAVITY OF OUR MISSION, SUPERMAN, BUT I CAN'T HELP REMEMBERING THAT WE'VE NEVER SETTLED WHICH OF US IS FASTER!
* THE GUARDIANS' POWER-DEVICES ARE NEUTRALIZED BY YELLOW!

WHILE WE'RE AT IT, WHY NOT MAKE THIS A RACE? WE'LL NEVER HAVE A BETTER OPPORTUNITY--
--AND MAYBE THE ELEMENT OF COMPETITION WILL SPUR US TO DO BETTER THAN OUR VERY BEST!
YOU'RE ON, FLASH!-- A RACE IT IS!

SO, MOMENTS LATER...
ON YOUR MARKS...
GET SET...
GO!

BEFORE THE BATMAN'S WORDS HAVE DIED, THE DUO IS PASSING LUNA...

QUITE A GIMMICK, THIS MEDALLION!-- IT FORMS A "RUNNING TRACK" IN FRONT OF ME AS I MOVE...

...AND TELEPATHICALLY SHOWS ME A MAP OF OUR ROUTE!

7

PAST MARS, JUPITER, SATURN, URANUS, NEPTUNE, PLUTO THEY STREAK... BEYOND THE BOUNDARIES OF THE SOLAR SYSTEM...

--WHILE, ON EARTH OF ALMOST TWO THOUSAND YEARS AGO, JIMMY OLSEN IS TAKEN BEFORE A ROMAN GENERAL...
E PLURIBUS UNUM! VENI VIDI VICI! CAVE CANEM!
NO USE! THESE GUYS ONLY SPEAK LATIN... AND I'VE FORGOTTEN MOST OF WHAT I LEARNED IN HIGH SCHOOL!
HERE IS THE MAGICIAN, EXCELLENCY!*
*NOTE: OUR RESIDENT LINGUIST HAS TRANSLATED THE ROMANS' SPEECH INTO ENGLISH FOR US!

HE VIRTUALLY REEKS EVIL! I ORDER AN EXECUTION! IMPRISON HIM UNTIL DAWN! THEN--DEATH!
I DON'T UNDERSTAND ALL HIS WORDS! BUT I RECOGNIZE HIS TONE... PURE NASTY!

TAKE HIM AWAY!
WHAT KIND OF MESS HAVE I STUMBLED INTO... AND HOW IN THUNDER DO I STUMBLE OUT AGAIN?!
8

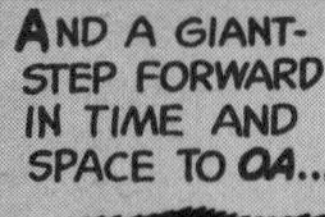
AND A GIANT-STEP FORWARD IN TIME AND SPACE TO OA...

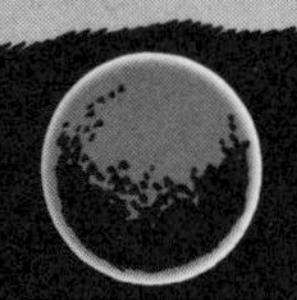

NOW THAT WE HAVE TAUGHT YOU OUR LANGUAGE, I CAN EXPLAIN-- SUPERMAN AND THE FLASH MUST TRAVERSE THE PERIMETERS OF OUR GALAXY--
-- AND THE NEIGHBORING CLUSTER OF STARS, ANDROMEDA!--IN A COUNTER-CLOCKWISE FASHION...

--THE OPPOSITE DIRECTION OF THE ANACHRONIDS! THEY MUST CROSS PRECISELY WHERE THE ALIENS HAVE BEEN--
THEY ARE NOW APPROACHING A DWARF STAR ABOUT 16 LIGHT-YEARS FROM EARTH!

THUS FAR, WE'RE NECK AND NECK! FLASH IS EASILY MY EQUAL WHEN IT COMES TO VELOCITY!
UNFORTUNATELY, HE ISN'T INVULNERABLE...
SOMETHING'S APPROACHING... SOMETHING... SOMETHING MOVING EVEN FASTER THAN WE ARE!

THOSE MUST BE... THE ANACHRONIDS!
WONDER WHAT THAT IS THEY'RE CARRYING--?

A WEAPON--! THE GUARDIANS DIDN'T SAY ANYTHING ABOUT THE ANACHRONIDS BEING HOSTILE!
9

GOT TO PUT MYSELF BETWEEN THEM AND MY BUDDY... AND HOPE THERE'S NO TRACE OF KRYPTONITE IN THOSE BOLTS!
GOOD! THEIR BLASTS ARE NO MORE HARMFUL TO ME THAN AN ORDINARY ARTILLERY SHELL!

IT'S INCREDIBLE THAT THEY CAN EVEN AIM... MOVING AT THAT VELOCITY! THE SPEED OF LIGHT WOULD BE A SNAIL'S CRAWL BY COMPARISON...
STILL, IF I REALLY POUR ON THE EFFORT, I MAY BE ABLE TO CATCH ONE...

GREAT KRYPTON--! I FORGOT ALL ABOUT THE FLASH! HE WAS KNOCKED OFF COURSE BY THE BLAST... HE'S STUNNED--
--AND HE'S PLUNGING TOWARD THAT SUN-- THAT YELLOW SUN...

HIS MEDALLION IS VULNERABLE TO YELLOW!
HE'LL EITHER BURN IN THE HEAT OF THE STAR... OR FREEZE IN SPACE... UNLESS I CAN GET TO HIM!

MADE IT! I'LL SHIELD HIM FROM THE YELLOW RAYS WITH MY CAPE UNTIL I FLY BACK ON COURSE!
10

I SEE IT NOW... THE ENERGY-BLASTS HAVE MADE THE SUN UNSTABLE...

...DISRUPTED THE REGULAR NUCLEAR CYCLES... AND IT'S GOING TO...

SUPER-NOVA!!

SUPER-NOVA... THE MOST AWESOME OF STELLAR DISASTERS... THE EXPLOSION OF A STAR... THE RELEASE OF UNIMAGINABLE ENERGIES... RENDING AND TEARING AND BLASTING SPACE FOR MILLIONS OF MILES!

11

COME ON, FLASH... OUR ONLY CHANCE IS TO OUTRUN THE SHOCK-WAVES!
YOU DON'T HAVE TO CONVINCE ME, CHUM!
I HEARD SUPERMAN TALK! EVIDENTLY, THE MEDALLION ALSO ENABLES US TO SPEAK IN AIRLESS SPACE!

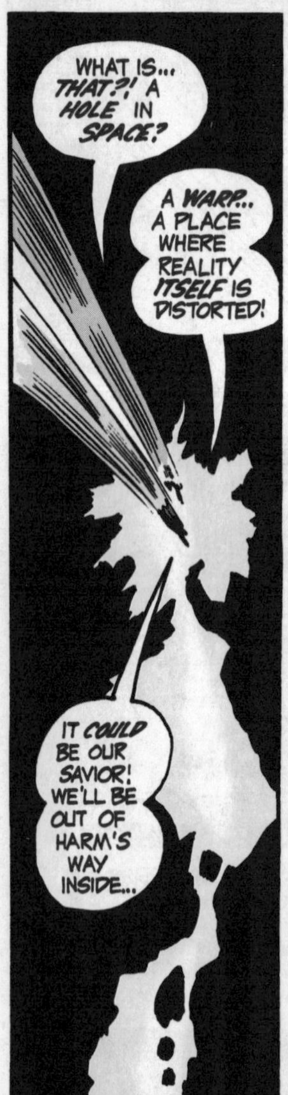
WHAT IS... THAT?! A HOLE IN SPACE?
A WARP... A PLACE WHERE REALITY ITSELF IS DISTORTED!
IT COULD BE OUR SAVIOR! WE'LL BE OUT OF HARM'S WAY INSIDE...

SUPERMAN--! WHERE ARE WE...? I CAN'T TELL UP FROM DOWN!
ME EITHER! THIS IS A DIFFERENT SPACE-TIME PLANE... ANOTHER DIMENSION!
NOTHING WE CAN DO TILL WE STOP FALLING... EXCEPT PRAY!

FLASH HAS DRIFTED AWAY FROM ME... I CAN ONLY HOPE WE COME OUT OF THIS THING NEAR ONE ANOTHER!
I SEEM TO BE EMERGING ON SOME SORT OF SOLID GROUND... A PLANET!
BUT WHICH PLANET-- AND WHERE!?
12

APPARENTLY WE BROKE THROUGH TO SOME ALTERNATE UNIVERSE!
THIS IS THE STRANGEST LAND-SCAPE I'VE EVER SEEN...AND THAT DOUGHNUT-SHAPED SUN ISN'T EXACTLY NORMAL EITHER!
I'D BETTER NOT STAND HERE GAWKING...

I'LL FIND FLASH AND-- HUH? THE SUN'S CHANGING COLOR... TO RED!

I LOSE MY SUPER-POWERS UNDER A RED SU... NNNGH!
THODD

AT LAST! OUR ARCH-ENEMY IS TOTALLY WITHIN OUR POWERS!
TAKE HIM TO... THE DEVOURERS!
WE SHALL HAVE THE PLEASURE OF WATCHING HIM DIE!

PERHAPS AN HOUR HAS PASSED... PERHAPS MERE SECONDS...

OW... I CAN PITY NON-SUPER MEN IF THEY HAVE TO PUT UP WITH THIS SORT OF PAIN...
SOMEBODY MUST'VE SLUGGED ME AND CARRIED ME HERE-- WHEREVER HERE IS!
SKNCH SKNCH SKNCH
13

GREAT KRYPTON-- WHAT SORT OF BEAST IS THAT?...A REFUGEE FROM A NIGHTMARE!

--A PARTICULARLY HORRIBLE NIGHTMARE! NO MATTER, THOUGH...
...THE SUN'S REVERTED TO YELLOW...SO I SHOULDN'T HAVE ANY TROUBLE--

MY HAND--! I'M TOO LATE! THE SUN TURNED RED AGAIN!

IT'S STRONG... DEVILISHLY POWERFUL! AS A NORMAL MAN, I CAN'T HOPE TO BATTLE IT!
IT'S PULLING ME TOWARD THAT...MOUTH!
--AND I... CAN'T... BREAK... LOOSE!

AT THAT INSTANT, A HUNDRED EARTH-MILES DISTANT...

THIS'S ONE BIG PLANET! I'VE ALREADY COVERED THE EQUIVALENT OF THREE EARTH-SIZE WORLDS...
...AND STILL NO SIGN OF SUPERMAN!
I'LL HAVE A GO AT THE TERRITORY BEYOND THOSE MOUNTAINS--
14

A PULSE-BEAT LATER...
SUPER-MAN... HELPLESS AS A KITTEN!

IT'S A CINCH I WON'T SAVE HIM WITH MY FISTS! THIS THING HAS A HIDE LIKE ARMOR-PLATE--

NO EYES...NO EARS... HOW DOES IT SENSE?
I CAN MAKE A GUESS...AND IT HAD BETTER BE GOOD!
THOSE WAVING STALKS MUST OPERATE LIKE RADAR-ANTENNAE--!

MAYBE IF I RAISE A DUST CLOUD, IT'LL INTERFERE WITH THE RADAR BEAMS...
CONFUSE THE BEAST FOR A FEW LIFE-SAVING MOMENTS!

IT'S WORKING! THE THING IS STUMBLING... NOW TO GO INTO PHASE TWO!
WHEN YOU JAM A THUMB INTO A HUMAN'S EYE, IT HURTS PLENTY!
15

MAYBE THIS WILL HAVE THE SAME EFFECT!
YEAH...RIGHT ON THE BUTTON! THE CREATURE'S HURTING... DROPPING SUPERMAN!

ANYTIME... YOU WANT A MONSTER TAKEN CARE OF, GIVE ME A CALL!
TH-THANKS...
I SEE THE SUN IS YELLOW AGAIN! BEFORE IT CHANGES ITS SOLAR MIND...

...I HAVE A LITTLE CHORE!
KA-SMAKKK

SWELL! SO MUCH FOR THE BEASTIE...NOW DO YOU HAVE ANY BRIGHT IDEAS ABOUT HOW WE RETURN TO OUR UNIVERSE?
EVERY SECOND WE SPEND HERE BRINGS IT CLOSER TO ITS ULTIMATE DOOM--
MATTER OF FACT, I DO HAVE AN IDEA! I THINK WE'RE LOOKING AT OUR "GATE-WAY" FROM BEHIND...
16

GATEWAY--? WHERE?
THERE-- RIGHT THROUGH THAT HOLE!

THROUGH THE SUN?! SUPERMAN, THAT SCUFFLE WITH THE MONSTER MUST'VE UNHINGED YOU! MAYBE YOU'D SURVIVE...
...BUT I'D BE BURNED TO A CINDER!
NOT IF YOU WENT THROUGH FAST ENOUGH! LOOK, IT'S KNOWN THAT SPACE AND TIME ARE DISTORTED NEAR BIG STARS...

I FIGURE THE ANACHRO-NIDS CAME FROM HERE-- I'LL EXPLAIN WHY LATER-- AND THAT'S THEIR DOOR TO OUR DIMENSION!
IT BETTER BE... SPACE-WARPS AREN'T RELIABLE!
ANYWAY, IT'S THE ONLY CHOICE WE HAVE!

OKAY, I'M GAME... I GUESS! LET'S GO... BEFORE I COME TO MY SENSES!

DON'T TRY IT TILL YOU'VE BUILT UP A VELOCITY OF AT LEAST TWICE THAT OF LIGHT--

WITH LUCK-- AND AT 372,000 MILES PER SECOND--WE'LL BE ON THE FAR SIDE BEFORE THE HEAT GETS TO US!

17

THUS DOES THE GALLANT PAIR GAMBLE ALL IN A SINGLE FRANTIC, DESPERATE EFFORT...
THEY HURL THEIR BODIES INTO THE HUNGRY HEART OF THE ATOMIC FURNACE THAT IS A STAR...
A WELTER OF GAS AND MATTER, BLAZING PER-PETUALLY AT A SURFACE TEMPERATURE OF 5,000 DEGREES... WITH A CORE 25,000,000 DEGREES HOT...
...A LIVING HELL NO MAN HAS EVER EXPERIENCED UNTIL THIS FATEFUL MOMENT--*
*EDITOR'S NOTE: OKAY, SUPERMAN HAS FLOWN INTO OUR SUN BEFORE... BUT IT DIDN'T KEEP CHANGING COLOR ON HIM!
18

...AND MIRACULOUSLY, EMERGE IN A FAMILIAR COSMOS!
MADE IT! YOUR GUESS AND A HEAP OF LUCK PULLED US THROUGH!
MORE LUCK THAN YOU KNOW! HALF-WAY, THE SUN CHANGED TO RED.. BUT I HAD ENOUGH MOMENTUM TO KEEP GOING!

ON OA...
THEY HAVE ESCAPED THEIR OTHER-DIMENSIONAL PRISON! ONCE MORE, THEY RESUME THE FATE-FUL RACE TO SAVE THE UNIVERSE...
THEY APPROACH THE GALAXY OF ANDROMEDA! AND BEHOLD! A CLUSTER OF ANACHRONIDS APPROACHES FROM THAT REGION!

MORE OF THOSE ALIENS ARE COMING OUR WAY!
SUPERMAN, WE DON'T EVEN KNOW WHAT WE'RE COMBATING! I MOVE WE SUSPEND OUR RACE LONG ENOUGH TO CAPTURE ONE--!

SECONDED! LET'S YANK OUT ALL THE STOPS...
...AND POUR IT ON!
19

I HATE TO BE IMMODEST.., BUT I DID CATCH ONE FIRST!
OKAY, YOU'RE FAST! MAYBE FASTER THAN I! BUT THAT GETS DECIDED LATER!

THIS CREEP DIDN'T GET THE MESSAGE! ITS RAY-GUN BLAST DOESN'T EVEN TICKLE!

WHEW IT'S SLIPPERY!
HANG ON! IT CAN'T KEEP UP THIS SPEED IF WE PULL IN THE OPPOSITE DIRECTION!

IT'S SLOWING... STOPPING! WE MAKE A FINE PAIR OF ANCHORS!
AM I WRONG-- OR IS THIS SOME KIND OF ROBOT?!

SEEMS TO BE... FLASH-- GET AWAY!
HUH? I CAN'T SEE ANY DANGER--
20

IT'S... DISINTE-GRATING?!
I'LL HAVE TO TRY ANOTHER GUESS... AND THEORIZE IT CAN'T EXIST AT THE SPEEDS WE THINK OF AS "NORMAL"!

IT WAS DESIGNED TO FUNCTION ONLY AT LIGHT-PLUS VELOCITY!
DESIGNED-- BY WHOM? YOU KNOW SOME-THING I DON'T?
I'M NOT SURE... BUT I CERTAINLY HAVE A BUSHEL OF MORE GUESSES!

NOTHING THAT'S HAPPENED IS NATURAL! SOMEBODY'S BEHIND IT ALL... THERE'S A DEFINITE PLOT!
...ONLY I HAVEN'T FATHOMED THE REASON--YET!
MEANWHILE, WE'D BETTER KEEP MOVING... THERE'S A LOT OF ANACHRONIDS LOOSE-- AND THEY'RE STILL DISRUPTING THE TIME FLOW!

LAST ONE TO THE FAR SIDE OF ANDROMEDA IS A ROTTEN APPLE...
IT CONTINUES, THEN... THE MAD DASH ACROSS THE COSMOS! FOR THE MOMENT, SUPERMAN AND FLASH ARE SAFE--FREE TO CONCENTRATE ON THEIR MONUMENTAL TASK!
21

JIMMY OLSEN, TRAPPED IN THE YEAR 15 B.C., IS NOT SAFE, HOWEVER...
THE BARBARIANS GATHER ON THE FAR SIDE OF THE RIVER! WE CLASH WITH THEM AT SUNRISE...
THEREFORE, THE EXECUTION OF THE SPY CANNOT WAIT! IT MUST PROCEED IMMEDIATELY!
I WISH YOU GUYS WOULD SPEAK ENGLISH... BUT THAT LANGUAGE DOESN'T EXIST YET!

I FEEL LIKE THE MAIN ATTRACTION AT A FISH-FRY-- THE FISH!

--AND IT LOOKS LIKE I'M ABOUT TO BE HOOKED!
LISTEN, YOU JUNIOR-LEAGUE GREEN ARROWS... DON'T I EVEN GET A JURY TRIAL?

NO USE...THEY WON'T LISTEN... THEY CAN'T UNDERSTAND!
MY SIGNAL-WATCH, CAN'T CALL SUPERMAN THROUGH TIME! HE WON'T BE AROUND TO PULL OFF A LAST-MINUTE SAVE...

THE BOW-STRINGS TWANG... AND FIVE DEADLY SHAFTS SPRING ACROSS THE CLEARING TOWARD THE HAPLESS FRIGHTENED REPORTER!

IN A MICRO-SECOND, JIMMY OLSEN WILL KNOW HIS FATE! BUT YOU WILL HAVE TO WAIT FOR OUR NEXT ISSUE FOR THE MOST DRAMATIC AND SURPRISING CLIMAX IN THE ANNALS OF SUPERMAN AND THE FLASH!

22

WORLD'S FINEST COMICS
DC WORLD'S FINEST
presents
SUPERMAN and THE FLASH
APPROVED BY THE COMICS CODE AUTHORITY
DEC. NO. 199
15¢
HERE THEY COME!
FINISH LINE
I CAN'T BELIEVE IT! MY HERO-- LOST!
YAY! MY HERO WON!

OFTEN HAVE THE MIGHTY SUPERMAN AND THE INCREDIBLE FLASH
PERFORMED AWESOME DEEDS! BUT NONE SO AWESOME AS THIS--A RACE AROUND TWO VAST GALAXIES, TO COUNTERACT THE TIME-DISRUPTING EFFECTS OF THE FASTER-THAN-LIGHT ANACHRONIDS...
...WHILE NEWSHOUND JIMMY OLSEN, IMPRISONED 2000 YEARS IN THE PAST, IS ABOUT TO DIE IN A HAIL OF ROMAN ARROWS--!
HANG ON... BECAUSE FROM HERE FORWARD OUR STORY MOVES ALMOST AS BLINDINGLY QUICK AS OUR HEROES! FOLLOW THEM INTO ASTONISHING PERILS AS THEY MEET IN A DESPERATE...
RACE TO SAVE TIME
A "WORLD'S FINEST" GIFT FROM...
DENNY O'NEIL--WRITER
DICK DILLIN & JOE GIELLA--ARTISTS
JULIUS SCHWARTZ--EDITOR
S-533
1

EVEN AS THE IRON-BARBED SHAFTS NEAR THEIR MARK, THE BEWILDERED REPORTER'S BODY SEEMS TO MELT--
WHEW! I'M DOING MY DISAPPEARING ACT AGAIN... AND NOT A MOMENT TOO SOON!

AFTER A MOMENT OF NON-EXISTENCE, JIMMY SHIMMERS INTO SOLIDITY ELSEWHERE--
DON'T KNOW WHERE I AM... BUT ANYPLACE WILL BE AN IMPROVEMENT OVER THE CAMP OF THOSE ARROW-HAPPY SOLDIERS!

AIEEEE--! WHAT FURTHER PROOF OF HIS GUILT DO YOU REQUIRE, ESTEEMED JUDGE?
BEFORE YOUR OWN EYES, HE VANISHED AND REAPPEARED IN ANOTHER FORM!
OBOY... I DIDN'T JUMP FROM THE FRYING PAN INTO THE FIRE--JUST ANOTHER FRYING PAN!

I RECOGNIZE THIS PLACE FROM ETCHINGS IN HISTORY BOOKS! IT'S THE STAR CHAMBER OF THE SPANISH INQUISITION!
SOMEHOW, I'VE JUMPED AHEAD IN TIME OVER 1400 YEARS... AND APPARENTLY I'VE TAKEN THE PLACE OF A MAN ACCUSED OF WITCHCRAFT!
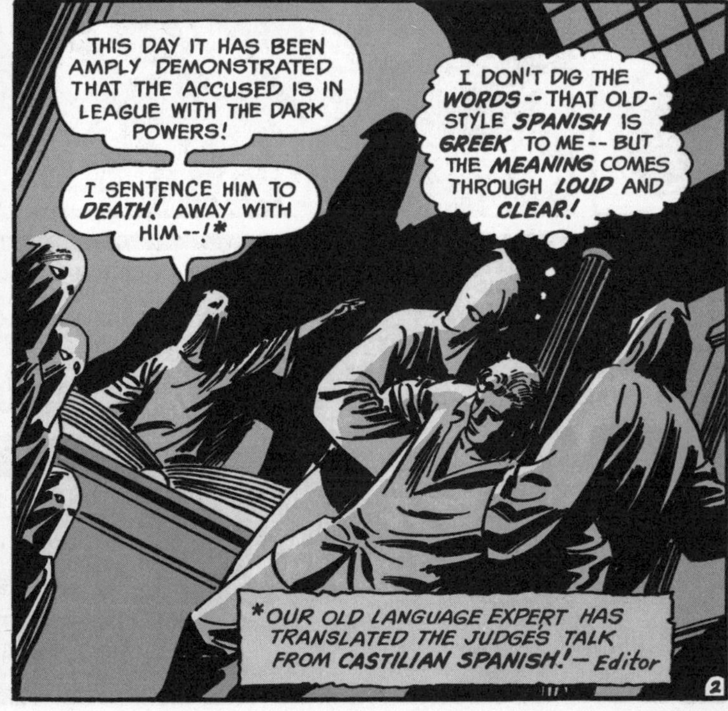
THIS DAY IT HAS BEEN AMPLY DEMONSTRATED THAT THE ACCUSED IS IN LEAGUE WITH THE DARK POWERS!
I SENTENCE HIM TO DEATH! AWAY WITH HIM--!*
I DON'T DIG THE WORDS--THAT OLD-STYLE SPANISH IS GREEK TO ME--BUT THE MEANING COMES THROUGH LOUD AND CLEAR!
*OUR OLD LANGUAGE EXPERT HAS TRANSLATED THE JUDGE'S TALK FROM CASTILIAN SPANISH! — Editor
2

MEANWHILE, FIVE CENTURIES LATER AND UNCOUNTED LIGHT-YEARS AWAY--

WE'VE LEFT OUR OWN *MILKY WAY GALAXY*... AND ARE APPROACHING THE NEIGHBORING *ANDROMEDA GALAXY!*

SO FAR, WE'RE RE-TRACING THE PATH OF THE *ANACHRONIDS EXACTLY!* I HOPE THE *GUARDIANS'* SCHEME IS *WORKING!*

IT IS, INDEED... FOR, ON *OA*, PLANETARY HOME OF THE IMMORTAL *GUARDIANS*...

THUS FAR, ALL IS WELL! DESPITE A BRIEF STAY IN ANOTHER DIMENSION, THE TERRANS *SUPERMAN* AND *FLASH* ARE PROCEEDING AS PLANNED!
THERE HAS BEEN BUT A *MINOR* SHIFT IN THE TIME-LINE!*
*NOTE: AND THAT TIMELY SHIFT SAVED JIMMY'S LIFE... FOR THE MOMENT!

WHEN THIS GALLANT PAIR HAS COMPLETED A *REVERSE CIRCUIT* OF THE PATH OF THE *ANACHRONIDS*, COMPLETE ORDER WILL BE RESTORED!
IN THE MEANTIME, THE *MEDALLION* WE GAVE *THE FLASH* -- THAT WHICH ENABLES HIM TO LIVE, RUN AND COMMUNICATE IN THE VACUUM -- IS DRAINING *ALL* OUR POWER-BROADCASTS!
UNTIL IT IS RETURNED TO US, OUR OWN *GREEN LANTERN CORPS* IS *HELPLESS!*

WITH THIS HANDY SUMMARY OF ALL THAT HAPPENED IN OUR *LAST* ISSUE OUT OF THE WAY, WE MOVE AHEAD WITH OUR MIND-BOGGLING ADVENTURE... BEGINNING AT THE TOP OF THE NEXT PAGE!

3

IN DEEPEST SPACE...
ODD... SUPERMAN LOOKS LIKE HE'S... SICK!
YOU OKAY, PAL?
I FEEL... WEAK!

ANY IDEA WHAT'S WRONG?
IT'S THAT ORANGE SUN! IT PUTS OUT LESS ENERGY THAN EARTH'S YELLOW SUN, SO MY POWERS ARE WEAKENED!

NOT TOO MUCH, I HOPE... HERE COMES ANOTHER FLOCK OF ANACHRONIDS!
...HEADING STRAIGHT FOR US--!

LOOKS LIKE A MASS ATTACK!

UNNGH! THAT HURT! I REALLY AM WEAKER...!

4

THERE MUST BE A HUNDRED OF THEM!
YEAH... AND MY FIST ISN'T DOING TOO WELL AGAINST THEIR METAL HIDES!

WE CAN'T LET THEM WIN...
... THE FATE OF HUMANITY IS RIDING ON US!

WE'VE GOT TO KEEP SLUGGING... UNN--!
SUPERMAN'S UNCONSCIOUS... OR WORSE! IT'S UP TO ME NOW--!

MY STRENGTH IS IN MY SPEED... AND THAT'S USELESS AGAINST THINGS THAT CAN EASILY MATCH IT!
IN THIS SITUATION, I'M NO MORE A SUPER-HERO THAN ANY ORDINARY MAN--
--AND I NEED TO BE MORE THAN ORDINARY... MUCH MORE--!
5

THEY'RE HAULING SUPERMAN AWAY BY THE CAPE! I MUST STOP...

ONE OF THEM HAS CAUGHT MY MEDALLION-CHAIN... TWISTING IT... PULLING ME ALONG!
GASP I... CAN'T... BREATHE--!
THUS DO THE VALIANT FALL...AND ARE WHISKED AWAY INTO A BLACKNESS WHERE NO MORTAL HAS YET GONE...

WHILE FIVE CENTURIES AGO...
LAST TIME, WITH THE ROMANS, I PLAYED IT SWEET... LET MYSELF BE LED LIKE A MEEK LITTLE LAMB!
AND IT ALMOST GOT ME VENTILATED!

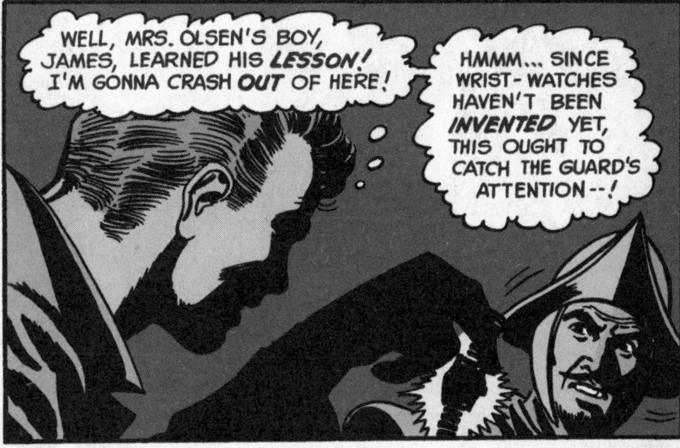
WELL, MRS. OLSEN'S BOY, JAMES, LEARNED HIS LESSON! I'M GONNA CRASH OUT OF HERE!
HMMM... SINCE WRIST-WATCHES HAVEN'T BEEN INVENTED YET, THIS OUGHT TO CATCH THE GUARD'S ATTENTION--!

SEE... GOES TICK-TOCK! PRETTY SWELL, HUH? AND CATCH THAT POINTER SPINNING AROUND THE DIAL--
6

AS I HOPED... HE'S COMPLETELY FORGOTTEN ABOUT ME!
I HAVEN'T USED THIS BODY-BLOCK SINCE I WAS SECOND-STRING LINEMAN ON THE HIGH SCHOOL FOOTBALL TEAM!
K-WOK

HE'LL BE OKAY... PROBABLY HAVE NO MORE THAN A BRUISE OR TWO!
I GOTTA FIND SOMEPLACE TO HIDE!

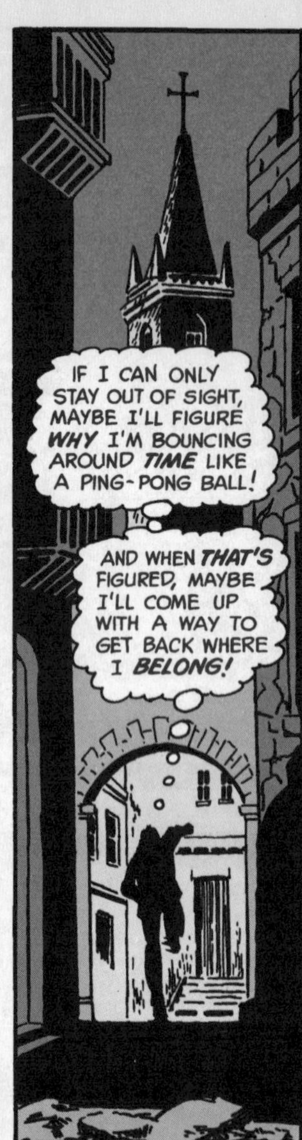
IF I CAN ONLY STAY OUT OF SIGHT, MAYBE I'LL FIGURE WHY I'M BOUNCING AROUND TIME LIKE A PING-PONG BALL!
AND WHEN THAT'S FIGURED, MAYBE I'LL COME UP WITH A WAY TO GET BACK WHERE I BELONG!

NOISE... LAUGHTER... COMING FROM THAT DOORWAY! MUST BE AN INN!
MAYBE I CAN GET A TEMPORARY JOB WASHING DISHES OR SOMETHING--!

AT LEAST IT'S WORTH A TRY--!
7

BUENAS DIAS... HUH — OH!
I GOOFED-- BAD!

DON'T PAY ANY ATTENTION TO ME, FELLAS! JUST GO ON WITH YOUR PARTY! I'LL STEP OUT FOR SOME FRESH AIR...
IT IS THE SORCERER! SEIZE HIM!

WHEN'LL I LEARN TO LOOK BEFORE I LEAP-- INTO TROUBLE!
THESE GUYS CAN REALLY RUN! BUT I SEE A SLIM CHANCE... THAT BALCONY AHEAD!

I'M MOMENTARILY OUT OF THEIR LINE OF VISION! GOTTA REACH THE ROOF FROM HERE AND--

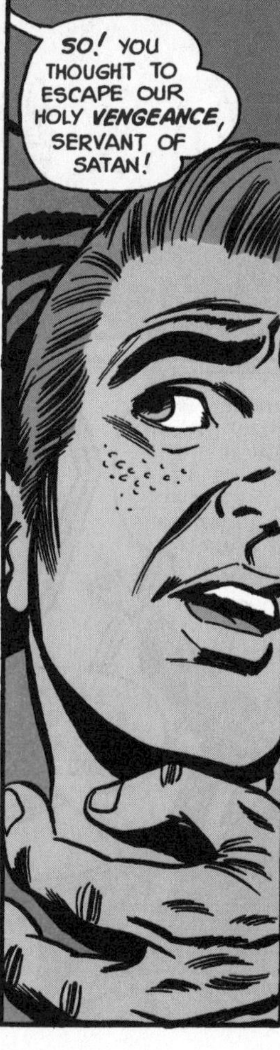
SO! YOU THOUGHT TO ESCAPE OUR HOLY VENGEANCE, SERVANT OF SATAN!

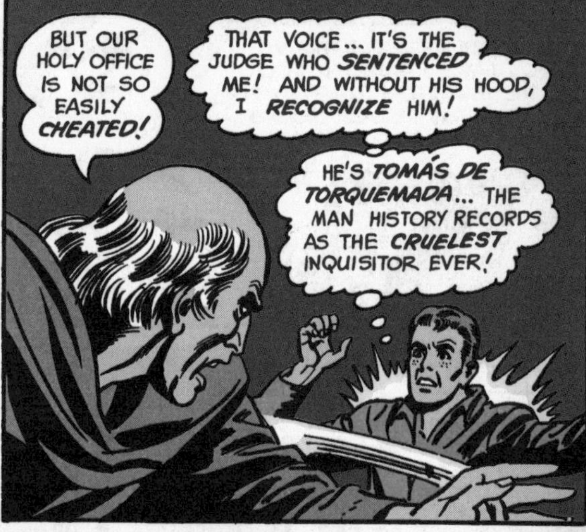
BUT OUR HOLY OFFICE IS NOT SO EASILY CHEATED!
THAT VOICE... IT'S THE JUDGE WHO SENTENCED ME! AND WITHOUT HIS HOOD, I RECOGNIZE HIM!
HE'S TOMÁS DE TORQUEMADA... THE MAN HISTORY RECORDS AS THE CRUELEST INQUISITOR EVER!

CONVEY HIM TO THE HEADSMAN!
JIMMY, MY LAD... YOU HAVE HAD IT!
8

NOR IS JIMMY THE ONLY ONE IN MORTAL DANGER... FOR, AS SUPERMAN AND THE FLASH SLOWLY REGAIN THEIR SENSES--

HA! OUR SLEEPING BEAUTIES AWAKE! I TRUST THEY ENJOYED THEIR NAP!

THE KRYPTONIAN KNOWS US... BUT PERHAPS WE SHOULD INTRODUCE OURSELVES TO HIS COMPANION! I AM KRU-EL!
AND I AM JAX-UR!
GENERAL ZOD, MILITARY GENIUS EXTRAORDINARY!
AND I AM THAT SCIENTIFIC WONDER, PROFESSOR VAKOX!

THESE ARE CRIMINALS... OUTLAWS PROJECTED INTO THE PHANTOM ZONE BY THE KRYPTON POLICE BEFORE MY HOME WORLD EXPLODED!
IS THIS WHERE WE ARE-- IN THE PHANTOM ZONE?!

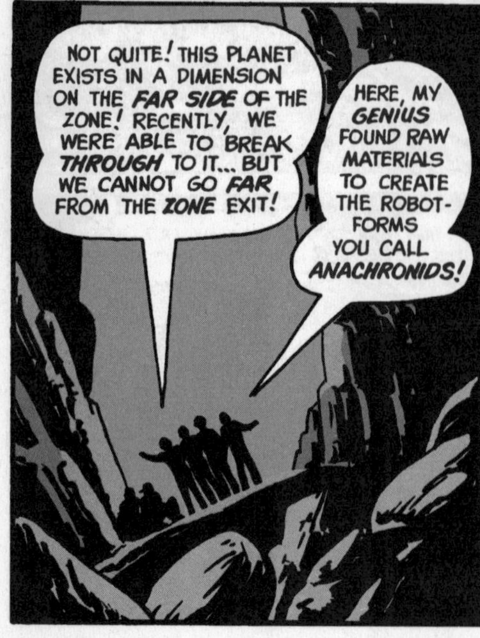
NOT QUITE! THIS PLANET EXISTS IN A DIMENSION ON THE FAR SIDE OF THE ZONE! RECENTLY, WE WERE ABLE TO BREAK THROUGH TO IT... BUT WE CANNOT GO FAR FROM THE ZONE EXIT!
HERE, MY GENIUS FOUND RAW MATERIALS TO CREATE THE ROBOT-FORMS YOU CALL ANACHRONIDS!

WE WERE ABLE TO SEND THEM THROUGH THE VORTEX OF THAT ODDLY-SHAPED SUN--A GATEWAY INTO YOUR DIMENSION!
I KNOW... WE ESCAPED THIS UNIVERSE VIA THE SAME ROUTE!*
*IT HAPPENED LAST ISSUE! --Editor
9

SO THE WHOLE THING IS A PLAN TO TRAP ME... FOR REVENGE!
YOU FLATTER YOURSELF, KAL-EL! REVENGE IS MERELY A PLEASANT BYPRODUCT!
INDEED! YOU SEE, WHEN THE ANACHRONIDS UPSET THE TIME STREAM, THE BARRIER BETWEEN THE PHANTOM ZONE AND EARTH'S SOLAR SYSTEM WILL SUNDER!
AND WE SHALL BE FREE, TO RULE WHAT IS LEFT OF THE UNIVERSE!

YOU'RE WILLING TO SACRIFICE BILLIONS OF LIVES... JUST TO FREE YOURSELVES?
CERTAINLY! THOSE BILLIONS MEAN NOTHING TO US!
MY CALCULATIONS SHOW THAT THE SUN WILL REMAIN RED FOR THE NEXT SEVEN EARTH-HOURS-- A PITY THAT SUPERMAN IS POWERLESS BENEATH RED RAYS!
WE WILL PERMIT YOU TO LIVE UNTIL OUR TASK IS ACCOMPLISHED!

WE'VE GOT TO GET LOOSE! CAN'T YOU VIBRATE THROUGH THESE BONDS?
HUH-UH! THEY TOOK THE GUARDIANS' MEDALLION--AND IT WAS SUPPLYING ME WITH ENERGY!
WITHOUT IT, I'M MUCH TOO EXHAUSTED! HOW ABOUT YOU?

I'LL... TRY... NO GOOD!
I'VE BEEN TOO WEAKENED... I'M TIED TOO TIGHT... AND THESE CABLES AROUND US ARE MADE OF A STRONG ALLOY-- THAT CAN'T BE BROKEN!
10

LOOK--! THEY LEFT THE GUARDIANS' MEDALLION HANGING ON THAT ROCK! I'VE AN IDEA-!
IT BETTER BE A CORKER!

AT THAT INSTANT, IN METROPOLIS--
LOOK, PERRY... AN OLD-FASHIONED TROLLEY CAR! THEY QUIT USING THOSE BEFORE I WAS BORN!
5¢
HMPF! MUST BE AN ADVERTISING STUNT!

...AND IN GOTHAM CITY...
I SAY, MASTER BRUCE! ISN'T THAT RUDOLPH VALENTINO? HE DIED OVER 40 YEARS AGO! I BELIEVE WE CAME TO SEE MR. PETER FONDA!
MUST BE A MIX-UP, ALFRED...

...AND IN DIANA PRINCE'S BOUTIQUE--
THIS IS ODD, CHING! I COULD'VE SWORN I HAD MINISKIRTS ON DISPLAY... NOT THESE ANTIQUES!
THIS OLD ONE DETECTS SINISTER VIBRATIONS, DIANA!
AMUSING INCIDENTS?
FAR FROM IT...!
11

...FOR, ON THE WORLD OF OA...

AGAIN, THE TERRANS HAVE PASSED FROM OUR DIMENSION! THE ANACHRONIDS ARE RAMPANT--
TIME CONVERGES, AND DOUBLES BACK UPON ITSELF! THINGS FROM THE PAST APPEAR IN THE PRESENT--

--UNLESS SUPERMAN AND FLASH REAPPEAR TO COMPLETE THEIR MISSION, THE UNIVERSE WILL DISSOLVE IN CHAOS!

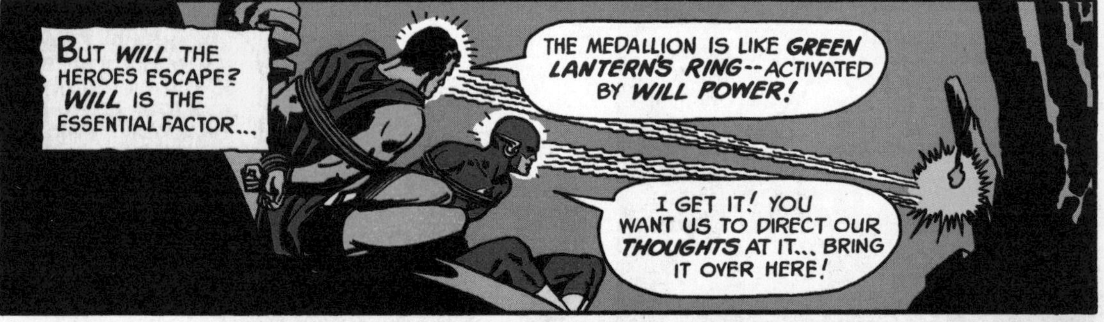

BUT WILL THE HEROES ESCAPE? WILL IS THE ESSENTIAL FACTOR...
THE MEDALLION IS LIKE GREEN LANTERN'S RING--ACTIVATED BY WILL POWER!
I GET IT! YOU WANT US TO DIRECT OUR THOUGHTS AT IT... BRING IT OVER HERE!

PULLED BY THE HEROES' COMBINED MENTAL COMMANDS, THE GREEN TALISMAN INCHES THROUGH THE ALIEN DUST-- SLOWLY, VERY SLOWLY...

AND THEN--
GOT IT! SO FAR, SO GOOD... NOW TO PERSUADE IT TO UNTIE US!
GREEN LANTERN SAYS IT HELPS TO VISUALIZE WHAT YOU WANT A POWER RING TO DO--PICTURE IT IN YOUR IMAGINATION!
12

OKAY, FLASH-- I'LL PICTURE A SAW--!
IT'S WORKING!

IT CUT THROUGH THE CABLES SMOOTH AS BUTTER!
HAVE IT DO THE SAME FOR ME!
NOT A CHANCE, TERRAN!

WE HAVE CHANGED OUR MINDS -- DECIDED YOU WERE MUCH TOO DANGEROUS TO LEAVE ALIVE, EVEN IN A WEAKENED CONDITION--
--A CORRECT DECISION, I SEE!

FIRST, I'LL DESTROY YOUR LITTLE TRINKET--
Z-HHHH

AND NEXT--YOU! I'M SORRY I HAVE NO FORMAL COURT-MARTIAL TO SANCTION YOUR EXECUTION--
IT WOULDN'T MAKE ANY DIFFERENCE, WOULD IT?
13

TAKE HIM, SUPERMAN!-- TAKE HIM GOOD!

A PUNY BLOW, KAL-EL! --I BARELY FELT IT!
MUST REMEMBER THAT I HAVE ONLY NORMAL POWER... I AUTO-MATICALLY PULLED MY PUNCH FOR FEAR OF KILLING HIM!

UNNGH
SEEMS THAT IF THERE'S ANY KILLING DONE --ZOD WILL DO IT!
--AND I'LL BE THE VICTIM!
KWOKK

AHHH... HOW GOOD YOUR FLESH FEELS AGAINST MY KNUCKLES!
ANOTHER ONE OF THOSE AND I'LL BE OUT...
FA-
WHMP

THE TROUBLE IS... I'M NOT USED TO EXTREME EFFORT! ORDINARILY, EVERYTHING IS EASY FOR ME--!
MUST--CONCENTRATE--ON GIVING IT ALL I'VE GOT!
14

HE'S GOING FOR HIS WEAPON... I CAN'T LET HIM REACH IT--

OWOO -- I MUST'VE TWISTED MY ANKLE IN THE JUMP... PAIN IS INTENSE!
CAN'T LET IT STOP ME, THOUGH... AT LEAST NOT TILL I GET THAT GUN!

DESPERATELY, THE ANTAGONISTS TWIST AND STRUGGLE BENEATH THE BLAZING RED SUN!

THEN, ***GENERAL ZOD'S*** FINGER JERKS ON THE TRIGGER... HIS BLASTER LEAPS AND SPITS A RAY OF DEATH TOWARD THE HELPLESS ***FLASH***...

WITH ONE FINAL, TREMENDOUS BURST OF EFFORT, ***SUPERMAN*** RAISES HIS FIST AND SLAMS THE EVIL GENERAL... AND THE FIGHT IS FINISHED!

YOU OKAY, FLASH?
NO SUCH LUCK... I CAUGHT THE EDGE OF THAT RAY... NOT ENOUGH TO HARM ME PERMANENTLY--

--BUT ENOUGH TO TEMPORARILY PARALYZE ME FROM THE WAIST DOWN! MY LEGS ARE USELESS!
AND I CAN'T PUT ANY WEIGHT ON MY ANKLE! WE'RE... CRIPPLED!

ZOD'S FOOTPRINTS LEAD THAT WAY! HE PROBABLY CAME FROM THE CONTROLS OF THE ANACHRONIDS--
IF WE CAN GET TO THEM, MAYBE--JUST MAYBE--WE CAN END THE MENACE TO THE UNIVERSE!
THEN LET'S START! WE CAN'T WALK...

...BUT WE CAN STILL CRAWL!
A GREAT PAIR OF WORLD-SAVERS WE ARE... SLITHERING ALONG LIKE BABIES!

CHEER UP... WE BEGAN THIS THING AS A RACE--REMEMBER? WELL, WE'RE STILL RACING--AND I'M STILL DETERMINED TO BEAT YOU!
16

AND, IN OLD SPAIN...

THAT BIG GOON'S GONNA MAKE SURE HIS AX DOES THE JOB! HE'S SHARPENING IT... AND IT'S ALREADY LIKE A RAZOR!
ZHHT-ZHHT

YOU SEE BEFORE YOU ONE WHO DARED DEFY OUR HOLY OFFICE... WHO LOOKED FROM OUR LIGHT TO DARKNESS!
LIKE ALL THOSE WHO CHOOSE THE PATH OF BLACK ARTS, HE MUST PAY--WITH HIS LIFE!

HE'S PROBABLY TELLING 'EM WHAT A SWELL FELLA HE IS... AND WHAT A SLOB I AM!
I'M INNOCENT, OF COURSE... BUT I HAVE A HUNCH THAT WOULDN'T MAKE ANY DIFFERENCE TO TORQUEMADA, EVEN IF HE BELIEVED ME!
HIS KIND GROOVE ON WHAT THEY CALL JUSTICE--BUT THAT'S ONLY A LABEL!

POWER AND FANATICISM ARE WHERE THEY'RE REALLY AT--!
AND THEY DIDN'T DIE OUT IN THE MIDDLE AGES... I CAN THINK OF A FEW TWENTIETH CENTURY TYPES EXACTLY LIKE 'EM!
LET US PRAY FOR THE CONDEMNED ...BEFORE WE DO OUR DUTY!

SURE, PRAY, YOU LOUSY HYPOCRITE... ONLY MAKE THOSE PRAYERS FOR YOURSELF--
--YOU NEED 'EM A LOT MORE THAN I DO!
17

WHILE JIMMY WAITS FOR THE LAST, EXCRUCIATING PAIN-- SUPERMAN AND THE FLASH, IN THE FAR FUTURE, COME WITHIN SIGHT OF THEIR OBJECTIVE...
THAT WEIRD SHACK MUST HOUSE THE ANACHRONID CONTROLS!
YES... BUT JAX-UR AND THE PROFESSOR ARE PLAYING 6-LAYER CHESS IN FRONT OF IT...

WE CAN'T RUSH THEM-- NOT IN THIS CONDITION...
BUT WE CAN TRY AN OLD, OLD TRICK...
WHEN I HEAVE THIS ROCK-- CRAWL, BUDDY... FAST AS YOUR HANDS AND KNEES WILL CARRY YOU!

THE SMALL STONE ARCS... LANDS WITH A DULL THUD AGAINST THE WALL OF THE STRUCTURE... AND...

WHAT WAS THAT?

OUR IMAGINATIONS-- OR PERHAPS A HARMLESS BEAST!

18

SEE THAT COUNTING GADGET OVER THE ENTRANCE?* ARE YOU THINKING WHAT I'M THINKING?
--THAT IT SHOWS HOW MANY SECONDS ARE LEFT BEFORE THE TIME-STREAM IN OUR UNIVERSE IS TOTALLY DISRUPTED?--YES!
WE HAVE LESS THAN A MINUTE! LET'S FINISH THAT RACE!
30
*OUR PICTORIAL-LINGUIST HAS TRANSLATED THE NUMERALS FROM KRYPTONESE, JUST FOR YOU -- Ed.

IT IS INSANE..! IT IS LUDICROUS..! AND, YES--IT IS *COMICAL!* THESE TWO RENOWNED WARRIORS DRAGGING THEMSELVES ON THEIR STOMACHS...

YET MARK THIS MOMENT WELL! FOR BEHOLD--THEY ARE INJURED, SHOCKS OF AGONY SCREAM ALONG THEIR LIMBS! AND STILL THEY GO FORWARD, FIRED BY THE MOST GALLANT DETERMINATION...

NEVER HAVE *SUPERMAN* AND *THE FLASH* STOOD SO *TALL*...

19

AND THE PRECIOUS SECONDS TICK AWAY....

AN ARM THAT SEEMS TO WEIGH A TON IS LIFTED... STIFF, ACHING FINGERS CLOSE OVER A MASTER SWITCH ... AND DRAG IT DOWN...

HEY! GUESS WHAT? I WON!
20

ALL OVER THE UNIVERSE, THINGS ABRUPTLY HAPPEN...

IN SPACE, THE ROBOTIC ***ANACHRONIDS*** SLOW, STOP...AND, UNABLE TO EXIST AT SUB-LIGHT VELOCITY, ***DISINTEGRATE***--

ORDER IS RESTORED TO THE STREAM OF TIME. IN MEDIEVAL SPAIN, JIMMY CHEATS THE EXECUTIONER AND FLASHES FORWARD TO HIS OWN ERA...

THE ROMAN SOLDIER DRIFTS ***BACK*** TO THE CAMP FROM WHICH HE WAS SNATCHED WHEN JIMMY FIRST DISPLACED HIM...

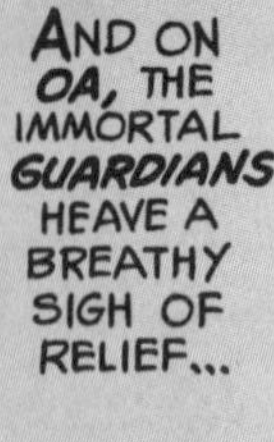

AND ON *OA,* THE IMMORTAL *GUARDIANS* HEAVE A BREATHY SIGH OF RELIEF...

I GUESS THAT SETTLES IT! I AM THE FASTEST MAN ALIVE!
ON THIS WORLD... THAT MUCH I'LL CONCEDE!
YOU HAVE DESTROYED OUR CAREFULLY WROUGHT ESCAPE!
YOU DIE!

OH, REALLY?
IT CAN'T BE! UNDER A RED SUN YOU ARE VULNERABLE!
ZHHHHHT

TRUE!... HOWEVER, THAT UNSTABLE SUN HAS JUST REVERTED-- TO YELLOW!
K-RUNCH

WHEN YOU WAKE UP, YOU'LL BE IMPRISONED WHERE YOU CAN'T ESCAPE! AND SINCE YOU'RE NOW SUPER, TOO, I NEEDN'T PULL MY PUNCH!
SWAT

I'LL MAKE CERTAIN THEY'LL NEVER USE THIS GADGET AGAIN! AND I'LL CHECK PERIODICALLY...
...TO INSURE THEY DON'T BUILD MORE ANACHRONIDS!
R-R-RIPP

I'VE FILLED MY LUNGS WITH AIR... I'LL LET IT OUT SLOWLY TO KEEP YOU ALIVE IN SPACE!
NOW, FLASH-- LET'S FLY THROUGH THAT GATE... BACK TO WHERE WE BELONG! THE GUARDIANS CAN THEN SEAL IT SO THE VILLAINS CAN'T ESCAPE!
THE END

THE LINE OF DC SUPER-STARS
LIMITED COLLECTORS' EDITION presents
THE GREATEST RACE OF ALL TIME!
$1.00
C-48
32161
SUPERMAN VS The FLASH
Extra: UNRELEASED PLANS of the FORTRESS OF SOLITUDE!
N-1618
2 FULL-LENGTH NOVELS GUEST STARRING THE JUSTICE LEAGUE!
HOW TO DRAW THE FLASH • 3D DIORAMA
PLUS OTHER SUPER-SPEED FEATURES!

YOU CAN TEAM UP WITH SUPERMAN! DETAILS INSIDE!

35¢

NO. 1

AUG.

31216

APPROVED BY THE COMICS CODE AUTHORITY

DC COMICS PRESENTS

SUPERMAN AND THE FLASH

CINEMA

FRANKENSTEIN

The MAN of STEEL and the SCARLET SPEEDSTER EMBARK ON A DEADLY "CHASE to the END OF TIME!"

Presenting--A BRAND-NEW SERIES--TEAMING SUPERMAN WITH DC'S MOST SENSATIONAL SUPER-STARS!

Garcia Lopez & DAN ADKINS

DC COMICS PRESENTS A BRAND-NEW SERIES OF ASTONISHING ADVENTURES-- TEAMING DC'S GREATEST HEROES WITH THE BIGGEST AND BEST OF THEM ALL... THE MAN OF STEEL...
IN THIS ISSUE:
SUPERMAN and THE FLASH
Created by JERRY SIEGEL & JOE SHUSTER
FOR YEARS, THE ACTION ACE AND THE SCARLET SPEEDSTER HAVE BEEN COLLEAGUES AND FRIENDS!
BUT BY A STARTLING TWIST OF FATE, THEY WILL SOON FIND THEMSELVES ON OPPOSITE SIDES OF A COSMIC STRUGGLE-- AS COMPETITORS ... AND ENEMIES!
YOU ARE NOW ENTERING ROSEMONT POP: 575
SOON, THE LANDING OF A UFO AND A STRANGE RAY FROM SPACE WILL TRIGGER A MIND-NUMBING CHAIN OF EVENTS... TURNING OUR STALWARTS INTO SUPER-BOUNTY HUNTERS WHO MUST EMBARK ON A DEADLY...
CHASE TO THE END OF TIME!
WRITER: MARTIN PASKO
ARTISTS: JOSE LUIS GARCIA-LOPEZ & DAN ADKINS
LETTERER: BEN ODA
COLORIST: JERRY SERPE
EDITOR: JULIUS SCHWARTZ

THE DESPERATE PURSUIT WHICH WILL CARRY SUPERMAN AND FLASH BEYOND THE FURTHEST REACHES OF MEASURABLE TIME WILL BEGIN IN A RURAL TOWN NAMED ROSEMONT...
...AS AN INDIRECT RESULT OF THE LANDING OF A MOST STRANGE SPACECRAFT...
...THE STRANGEST I'VE EVER SEEN!
MY MICROSCOPIC VISION SHOULD BE ABLE TO TELL ME WHAT IT'S MADE OF...
...BUT IT CAN'T POSSIBLY BE WHAT MY EYES REVEAL!
IT'S JUST TOO INCREDIBLE TO BELIEVE!
BY SWITCHING TO X-RAY VISION, I CAN BE SURE OF ONE THING, THOUGH...
...THAT THE SHIP IS EMPTY! IF IT EVER HAD A PILOT, HE'S GONE NOW, AND--
--EH? FEEL STRANGE--AS IF BEING HIT BY A WAVE OF SOME KIND!
I--I'M VIBRATING... NEARLY BEING SHAKEN APART--!
I'VE FLOWN INTO SOME SORT OF SUPER-TURBULENCE!
SO THAT'S IT... A RAY-- AND IT CAUSES ANYTHING IT HITS TO VIBRATE!
LOOKS LIKE IT'S COMING FROM OUT IN SPACE SOMEWHERE --BUT WHY?
2

THE ANSWER COMES WITH TERRIFYING SUDDENNESS-- PUNCTUATED BY A LOUD...
BANG
MEANWHILE-- JUST OUTSIDE ROSEMONT...
CENTRAL CITY IS ONLY A SECOND AWAY FROM HERE--IF YOU'RE THE FLASH, THAT IS!
SO WHEN THE POLICE RADIO ANNOUNCED THE SIGHTING OF A UFO HERE...
PARK
Holiday
Brandellis BA
COCKTAILS
HERTZ
HERTZ
...I FIGURED IT'D BE WORTH A SUPER-SPEED INVESTIGATION--
--HUNH? THAT WEIRD BEAM FROM OUT OF THE SKY-- HITTING THE TOWN...
...AND CAUSING IT TO VANISH--?!

CAR WASH
Car Wash
JOE'S
--SO, WITH A BURST OF YOUR HEAT VISION, YOU MELT THAT ALUMINUM ROOF...
THAT RAY IS PROBABLY CAUSING THE TOWN TO VIBRATE OUT OF THIS DIMENSIONAL PLANE--
...AND SHAPE IT INTO A GIANT SPATULA--TO SCOOP UP THOSE PEOPLE AND CARRY THEM OUT OF THE RANGE OF THE BEAM...
...SO THEY DON'T VANISH ALONG WITH THE TOWN? GOOD WORK!
NOT SO FAST--IT'S NOT OVER YET!
BUT IT WILL BE IF YOU PITCH IN, SPEEDSTER!
SINCE YOU'RE THE ONE WITH THE VIBRATORY POWERS--
--WHY DON'T YOU PUT THEM TO GOOD USE WHILE I'M OCCUPIED HERE?
YOU MEAN BY TRYING TO COUNTERACT THE "BAD VIBES"?
THAT'S JUST WHAT I WAS...
...THINKING OF DOING...
...ALL ALONG!
LIKE A HUMAN TORNADO, THE SULTAN OF SPEED CIRCLES THE TOWN...
4

...AND ALMOST INSTANTLY, THE SUPER-SPEED VIBRATIONS CANCEL OUT THOSE CREATED BY THE ALIEN RAY...
ROSEMONT'S STOPPED "FADING OUT"--WHICH LEAVES ME FREE TO INTERCEPT THE BEAM--
--AND TRACE IT TO ITS SOURCE...
WE GOT WHAT YOU NEED
...BY LITERALLY PUSHING IT BACK TO WHERE IT CAME FROM!
THE BEAM'S COMING FROM ONE OF THOSE TWO WARRING STARSHIPS! I'LL BET THEY'VE BEEN UP HERE FOR SOME TIME...
...SINCE THEY'RE FAR ENOUGH OUT TO ESCAPE THE EARLY-WARNING SYSTEMS OF U.S. SATELLITES!
THERE! NOW THAT I'VE FORCED THE RAY BACK INTO THE SHIP, I CAN--
?! GREAT SCOTT! THIS SHIP IS MADE OF THE SAME MATTER AS THE SMALLER CRAFT THAT EXPLODED!
NOW I'M FORCED TO ACCEPT WHAT MY MICROSCOPIC VISION SHOWED EARLIER!
IT'S UNBELIEVABLE --BUT TRUE!
5
BUT DISCOVERING WHAT THAT IS WILL HAVE TO WAIT-- BECAUSE, AT THE MOMENT, THE FASTEST MAN ALIVE IS WINDING UP HIS "RING-AROUND-ROSEMONT"...
WONDER HOW SUPERMAN'S MAKING OUT--?
YOU'LL FIND OUT SOON ENOUGH, FLASH...

...BECAUSE YOU'RE ABOUT TO *JOIN* HIM--THANKS TO YET *ANOTHER* STRANGE BEAM FROM ABOVE...
...WHICH CREATES A *FORCE-BUBBLE* AROUND YOU... LIFTING YOU *SKYWARD!*

WHILE IN *SPACE*...

THIS SHIP'S HULL IS COMPOSED OF *LIVING CELLS* -- MEANING THAT THESE "STARSHIPS" ARE ACTUALLY *LIVING ORGANISMS!*

IF THIS BLASTER-RAY HAD BEEN *ON-TARGET,* THE OTHER "SHIP" WOULD'VE BEEN *KILLED*--

--AND I *CAN'T ALLOW* THAT!

SUDDENLY, THE SHIP'S RAY-PROJECTOR *RETRACTS*... THE SLICK OUTER SURFACE OF THE SHIP *MUTATES*... AND A BIZARRE *VIEWING-SCREEN* SHIMMERS INTO EXISTENCE...

DESIST, ONE-NAMED-SUPERMAN!

MOONS OF KRYPTON! YOU--YOU'VE *ABDUCTED THE FLASH*--!

COMMUNICATING VIA SOME KIND OF *TELEPATHY*--?

DESIST AND... *BEHOLD!*

UNFORTUNATELY, MY SON--IT WAS *NECESSARY* ... FOR THE *PRESERVATION* OF THE *UNIVERSE!*

6

But before another thought can be telepathically "voiced"..
What?! You tricked me--?!
Again-- yes, it cannot be helped.
I am sorry, my son.

Suddenly, Superman finds his strength gone--and he can only watch helplessly as strange appendages grow out of the bows of the living ships...
...and slowly... gracefully... they glide toward one another...

...as if performing some weird ceremony ...a kind of cosmic mating ritual before their captive audience of one...
But the caped Kryptonian can see the maneuver for what it is --a docking in space...
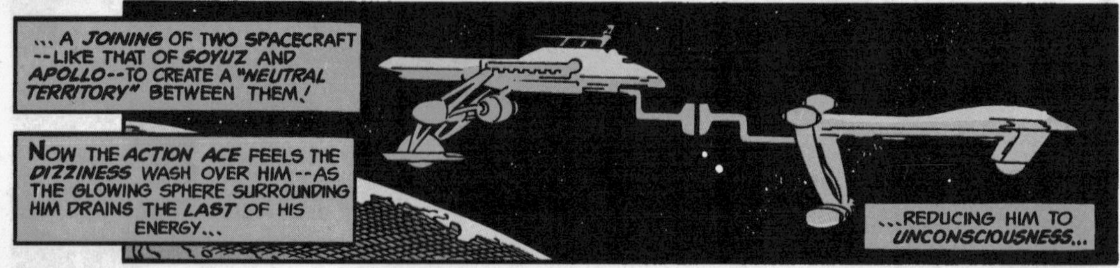
...a joining of two spacecraft --like that of Soyuz and Apollo--to create a "neutral territory" between them!
Now the Action Ace feels the dizziness wash over him--as the glowing sphere surrounding him drains the last of his energy...
...reducing him to unconsciousness...

...from which he is stirred by the strident voice of an alien martinet...
Welcome aboard, one-named-Superman. I am Islayn-- leader of the Volkir and captain of the vessel which captured you!
We are also responsible for the vibrational-beam which struck the place you call Rosemont!
7

THERE IS NO POINT IN ATTEMPTING TO ESCAPE YOUR CAGE, KRYPTONIAN... OR WOULD YOU PREFER TO BE CALLED SUPERMAN?

HOW INAPPROPRIATE THAT NAME SEEMS NOW! FOR YOUR PRISON IS FORMED OF Q-ENERGY*-- AGAINST WHICH YOU ARE POWERLESS!

*AN OTHER-DIMENSIONAL ENERGY WHICH AFFECTS SUPERMAN IN MUCH THE SAME WAY AS KRYPTONITE-- AND WAS FIRST ENCOUNTERED IN SUPERMAN #204 (FEB., 1968). --JULIE

DO FORGIVE US, MY SON-- WE AND THE VOLKIR DID WHAT WE FELT WAS NECESSARY!

"WE" ARE THE ZELKOT--THE SWORN ENEMY OF THE VOLKIR--AND I AM THE ZELKOT LEADER, AYLEM!

I--AH--"SPOKE" TO YOU JUST BEFORE YOU... "SURRENDERED"...

YOU MAY RECALL WE CAPTURED THE FLASH--?

BUT HE IS UNHARMED, SUPERMAN-- HE IS MERELY QUITE HELPLESS!

IT'S NO LIE, SUPERMAN! NOT EVEN I CAN GET OUT OF HERE!

THE MINUTE I TRY TO VIBRATE MY WAY THROUGH THE SCREENS THAT MAKE UP THE WALLS OF THIS CELL...

...THEIR MESH BECOMES DENSER-- IMPENETRABLE!

ALL RIGHT, ALL RIGHT! SO WE'RE YOUR PRISONERS!
NOW WHAT? DO YOU VOLKIR USE THAT BEAM AGAIN--AND FINISH DESTROYING EARTH?
OH, NO!
8
WE HAVE NO REAL INTEREST IN EARTH! WE MERELY CAME INTO THIS STAR-SYSTEM IN PURSUIT OF THE ZELKOT!
THEY LAUNCHED THAT ONE-PASSENGER CRAFT* WHICH LANDED IN ROSEMONT!
*THE ONE BACK ON PAGE ONE, REMEMBER? --JULIE

"WE ONLY SOUGHT TO KILL THE PILOT OF THAT CRAFT-- A ZELKOT REVOLUTIONARY NAMED IYLAR! SO WE DESTROYED HIS SHIP..."

"WE HAVE ONLY JUST LEARNED THAT IYLAR ESCAPED THE SHIP JUST BEFORE THE VIBRA-BEAM STRUCK IT!"

WE DID NOT INTEND TO CAUSE ROSEMONT'S DISAPPEARANCE! THAT WAS AN ACCIDENT! AT THIS DISTANCE FROM EARTH, THERE IS A TIME-LAG IN OUR SENSOR-RELAYS!
WE DID NOT DISCOVER THAT OUR VIBRA-BEAM HAD ACCOMPLISHED ITS TASK...
...UNTIL THE TOWN HAD NEARLY VANISHED!
THIS SORT OF THING HAPPENS CONSTANTLY! THE ZELKOT AND THE VOLKIR HAVE WARRED ACROSS THE UNIVERSE FOR BILLIONS OF EARTH-YEARS...
...AND THOSE PLANETS THAT ARE OCCASIONALLY CAUGHT IN THE MIDDLE OF OUR BATTLES ARE... WELL, DESTROYED!

SOUNDS LIKE YOU CERTAINLY DO A LOT OF CASUAL ANNIHILATING!
WHAT COULD BE SO IMPORTANT THAT YOU'RE WILLING TO HAVE ALL THOSE LIVES ON YOUR CONSCIENCE?
WHAT ARE YOU FIGHTING FOR?!
NOTHING.

WHAAT?!
WE FIGHT FOR...THE BATTLE ITSELF! WHICH IS TO SAY, THE REASON WE FIGHT IS LOST TO HISTORY!
WHATEVER STARTED OUR CIVIL WAR OCCURRED SO MANY GENERATIONS AGO, WE NO LONGER KNOW WHAT IT WAS!

"CIVIL WAR"--? I DON'T UNDERSTAND! YOU'RE TWO SEPARATE RACES--
YES... TODAY! ONLY AFTER MUCH EVOLUTION!
BUT ONCE WE WERE THE SAME RACE, MY SON... AND AS ONE UNITED PEOPLE--

LOOK, I COULDN'T CARE LESS ABOUT YOUR FAMILY TREE! GET TO THE POINT, WILL YOU?
AND IF YOU CALL ME "MY SON" ONE MORE TIME, I'LL--
AHH, BUT YOU ARE MY SON--IN A SENSE!
9

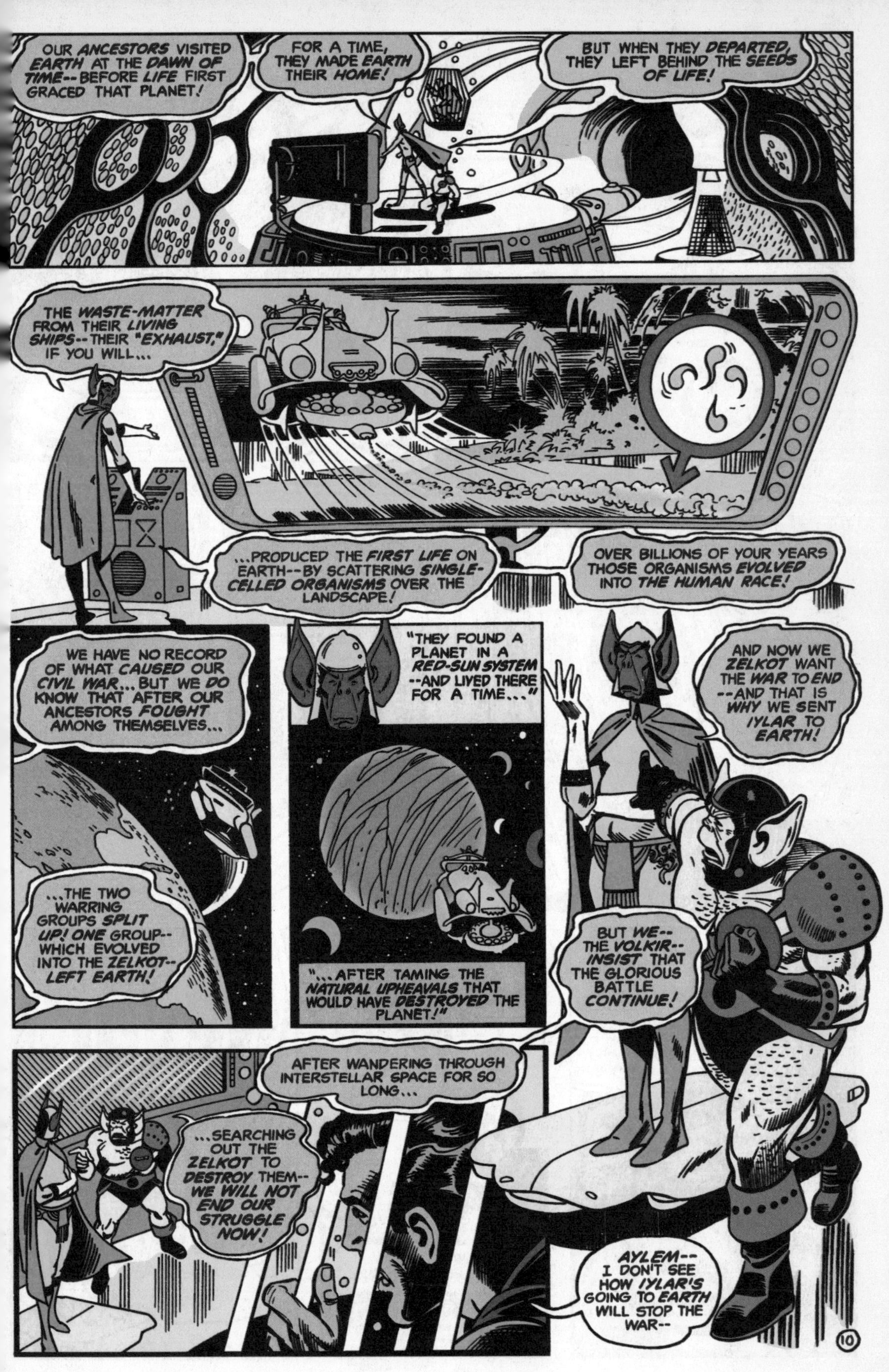

OUR ANCESTORS VISITED EARTH AT THE DAWN OF TIME-- BEFORE LIFE FIRST GRACED THAT PLANET!
FOR A TIME, THEY MADE EARTH THEIR HOME!
BUT WHEN THEY DEPARTED, THEY LEFT BEHIND THE SEEDS OF LIFE!
THE WASTE-MATTER FROM THEIR LIVING SHIPS-- THEIR "EXHAUST," IF YOU WILL...
...PRODUCED THE FIRST LIFE ON EARTH--BY SCATTERING SINGLE-CELLED ORGANISMS OVER THE LANDSCAPE!
OVER BILLIONS OF YOUR YEARS THOSE ORGANISMS EVOLVED INTO THE HUMAN RACE!
WE HAVE NO RECORD OF WHAT CAUSED OUR CIVIL WAR... BUT WE DO KNOW THAT AFTER OUR ANCESTORS FOUGHT AMONG THEMSELVES...
...THE TWO WARRING GROUPS SPLIT UP! ONE GROUP-- WHICH EVOLVED INTO THE ZELKOT-- LEFT EARTH!
"THEY FOUND A PLANET IN A RED-SUN SYSTEM --AND LIVED THERE FOR A TIME..."
"...AFTER TAMING THE NATURAL UPHEAVALS THAT WOULD HAVE DESTROYED THE PLANET!"
AND NOW WE ZELKOT WANT THE WAR TO END --AND THAT IS WHY WE SENT IYLAR TO EARTH!
BUT WE-- THE VOLKIR-- INSIST THAT THE GLORIOUS BATTLE CONTINUE!
AFTER WANDERING THROUGH INTERSTELLAR SPACE FOR SO LONG...
...SEARCHING OUT THE ZELKOT TO DESTROY THEM-- WE WILL NOT END OUR STRUGGLE NOW!
AYLEM-- I DON'T SEE HOW IYLAR'S GOING TO EARTH WILL STOP THE WAR--
10

NEVER MIND THAT! YOU WILL NOT LIVE LONG ENOUGH TO CONCERN YOURSELF WITH IT!
--NOR WILL THE FLASH-- FOR WITH A TOUCH OF THESE CONTROLS...
...I CAN CAUSE HIS CELL TO DIMINISH-- CRUSHING HIM!
AS IT DOES SO, ITS MESH BECOMES EVEN DENSER-- SO HE CANNOT HOPE TO ESCAPE!
AT THE SAME TIME...
...I INTENSIFY THE Q-ENERGY RADIATIONS OF YOUR CELL, SUPERMAN-- TO KILL YOU!
GASP THE PAIN-- AGONIZING! H-HOW CAN... A RACE AS... SEEMINGLY ADVANCED... AS PEACE-LOVING AS YOURS... GASP...
...DO SUCH A THING?
DO NOT MISTAKE THE ZELKOT, SUPERMAN--WE CAN BE RUTHLESS IF WE MUST!
SURELY WHEN YOU SAW OUR SHIPS JOIN TOGETHER, YOU MUST HAVE REALIZED...
...THAT THE ONLY REASON TWO SUCH MORTAL ENEMIES WOULD BAND TOGETHER...
...WOULD BE TO DESTROY A COMMON ENEMY!
YOU AND THE FLASH ARE THE ONLY TWO MEN ON EARTH WHO CAN THWART OUR PLANS!
AND WHILE AYLEM AND I SEEK DIFFERENT DESTINIES FOR OUR PEOPLE...
...WE ARE IN AGREEMENT ON ONE POINT:
WE WILL BROOK NO INTERFERENCE FROM OUTWORLDERS!
SO THIS... IS HOW IT ENDS, EH? WITH ME...
...REDUCED TO THIS-- FORCED TO ADMIT DEFEAT... MY STRENGTH... GONE--AND FLASH UNABLE TO ESCAPE A SLOW DEATH!
AND YOU CAN'T--CAN YOU, FLASH?
11

THAT CELL-- IT'S LIKE QUICKSAND... ISN'T IT, FLASH??!
POOR SUPERMAN-- HE'S IN SUCH PAIN, HE'S RAVING!
AND THROWING IN THE TOWEL THAT WAY--IT'S NOT LIKE HIM!
WAIT--MAYBE HE'S NOT BABBLING! HE DELIBERATELY EMPHASIZED THE WORD "QUICKSAND"!
HE'S TRYING TO SUGGEST A WAY TO ESCAPE-- WITHOUT THE ALIENS SUSPECTING!
QUICKSAND, HUNH? SURE--THE MORE YOU STRUGGLE AGAINST IT...

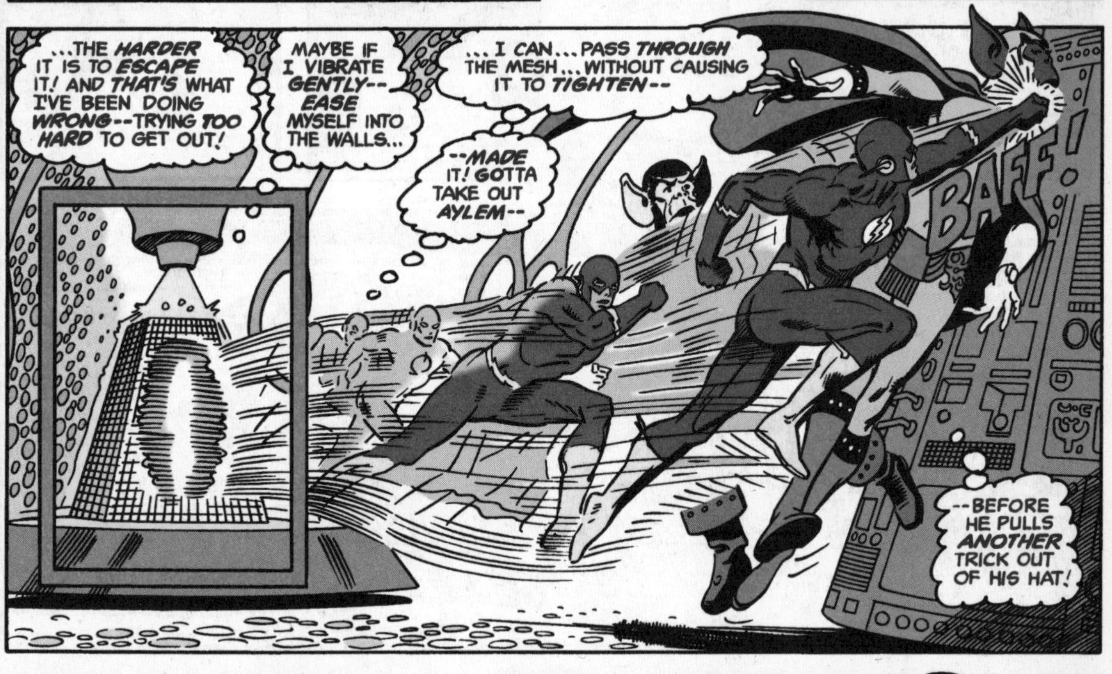
...THE HARDER IT IS TO ESCAPE IT! AND THAT'S WHAT I'VE BEEN DOING WRONG--TRYING TOO HARD TO GET OUT!
MAYBE IF I VIBRATE GENTLY-- EASE MYSELF INTO THE WALLS...
...I CAN...PASS THROUGH THE MESH...WITHOUT CAUSING IT TO TIGHTEN--
--MADE IT! GOTTA TAKE OUT AYLEM--
BAFF!
--BEFORE HE PULLS ANOTHER TRICK OUT OF HIS HAT!

AND BEFORE THE STUNNED ISLAYN CAN REACT...
CHOOM
...THE SCARLET SPEEDSTER CUTS THE Q-ENERGY SURROUNDING SUPERMAN WITH A SUPER-FAST MOVEMENT OF HIS HAND, AND...
12

KRAMM

NOW, *ISLAYN*-- YOU CAN *JOIN* YOUR "MORTAL ENEMY"... IN A *LONG NAP!*

WITH A STRANGLED CRY, *ISLAYN FALLS...*

...AND WHEN THERE IS NO FURTHER SOUND SAVE FOR THE HUSHED THROBBING OF THE LIVING SHIP...

THANKS, SPEEDSTER-- FOR MY *LIFE!*

DON'T THANK *ME,* PAL... IT WAS *YOUR* IDEA THAT SAVED-- *HUNH?*

DO NOT MOVE-- EITHER OF YOU!

--OR I PROMISE YOU, YOUR PLANET WILL *DIE!*

WHAT?!

?! APPARENTLY, *AYLEM* HAD A *CREW* WE--AH-- *DIDN'T KNOW* ABOUT!

YOU HAVE AMPLY DEMONSTRATED YOUR *POWERS,* EARTHERS -- AND WE ARE CONVINCED IT WOULD BE FUTILE TO *FIGHT* YOU!

VIBRATIONAL BEAM CONTROL*

HOWEVER, WE HAVE AN *ALTERNATIVE*-- *YOU WILL WORK FOR US!**

*TRANSLATED FROM THE *ZELKOTIAN* LANGUAGE.--*JULIE*

IF YOU THINK *I'M* GOING TO *HELP* YOU, YOU'RE--

OUR STUDIES OF EARTH HISTORY REVEAL THAT *HE* IS THE FASTER OF YOU TWO!*

SILENCE! I WAS *NOT* ADDRESSING *YOU!* IT IS *THE FLASH* WHO IS OF USE TO US!

**FLASH* WAS PROVEN FASTER THAN *SUPERMAN--SORT* OF-- IN *WORLD'S FINEST* #199 (DEC. 1970). --*JULIE*

"*AYLEM* TOLD YOU OF OUR COMRADE *IYLAR*-- WHO ESCAPED HIS SHIP'S DESTRUCTION? EVEN AS WE SPEAK, *IYLAR* IS JOURNEYING THROUGH *TIME!*"

3151 3102 3090 3078 2980 2240 2130 2025 1978

"YOU SEE, *IYLAR* WILL NOT *END* OUR CIVIL WAR, EXACTLY --HE WILL *PREVENT* IT!"

13

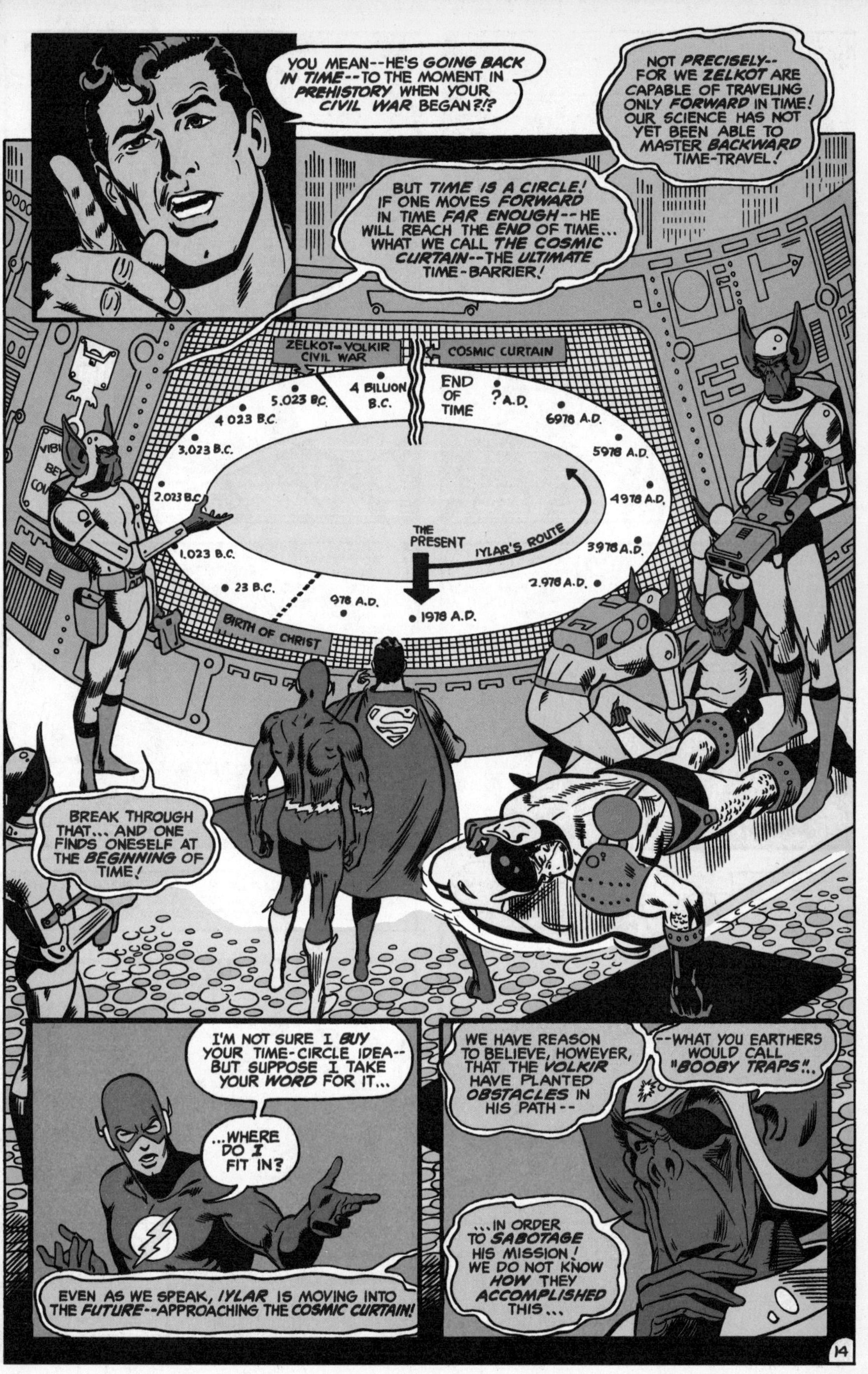

YOU MEAN--HE'S GOING BACK IN TIME--TO THE MOMENT IN PREHISTORY WHEN YOUR CIVIL WAR BEGAN?!?
NOT PRECISELY-- FOR WE ZELKOT ARE CAPABLE OF TRAVELING ONLY FORWARD IN TIME! OUR SCIENCE HAS NOT YET BEEN ABLE TO MASTER BACKWARD TIME-TRAVEL!
BUT TIME IS A CIRCLE! IF ONE MOVES FORWARD IN TIME FAR ENOUGH--HE WILL REACH THE END OF TIME... WHAT WE CALL THE COSMIC CURTAIN--THE ULTIMATE TIME-BARRIER!
ZELKOT-VOLKIR CIVIL WAR
COSMIC CURTAIN
4 BILLION B.C.
END OF TIME
? A.D.
5,023 B.C.
4,023 B.C.
3,023 B.C.
2,023 B.C.
1,023 B.C.
23 B.C.
978 A.D.
1978 A.D.
2,978 A.D.
3,978 A.D.
4,978 A.D.
5978 A.D.
6978 A.D.
THE PRESENT
IYLAR'S ROUTE
BIRTH OF CHRIST
BREAK THROUGH THAT... AND ONE FINDS ONESELF AT THE BEGINNING OF TIME!
I'M NOT SURE I BUY YOUR TIME-CIRCLE IDEA-- BUT SUPPOSE I TAKE YOUR WORD FOR IT...
...WHERE DO I FIT IN?
EVEN AS WE SPEAK, IYLAR IS MOVING INTO THE FUTURE--APPROACHING THE COSMIC CURTAIN!
WE HAVE REASON TO BELIEVE, HOWEVER, THAT THE VOLKIR HAVE PLANTED OBSTACLES IN HIS PATH--
--WHAT YOU EARTHERS WOULD CALL "BOOBY TRAPS"!..
...IN ORDER TO SABOTAGE HIS MISSION! WE DO NOT KNOW HOW THEY ACCOMPLISHED THIS...
14

...BUT OBVIOUSLY WE ARE IN NO POSITION TO DOUBT THEM! THUS WE WANT YOU, FLASH, TO SPEED INTO THE FUTURE...
...CATCH UP WITH IYLAR... AND ASSIST HIM SAFELY THROUGH THE COSMIC CURTAIN--
--TO ENSURE THE SUCCESS OF HIS MISSION!

REFUSE-- AND THAT CREWMAN WILL TURN THE VIBRA-BEAM ON EARTH--INSTANTLY DISINTEGRATING IT!
VIBRATIONAL BEAM CONTROL
NOT MUCH OF A CHOICE, IS IT? ALL RIGHT, I'LL DO IT--
--I HAVE TO!

VERY WELL! WEAR THIS--IT IS A COMMUNICATIONS-DEVICE! IT WILL PERMIT YOU TO REMAIN IN CONTACT WITH US ACROSS TIME!
WE WILL RETURN YOU TO EARTH-- AND FROM THERE, YOU CAN PROCEED INTO THE FUTURE!

OH, AND ONE MORE THING: IF YOU ARE NOT SUCCESSFUL IN KEEPING IYLAR FROM HARM...
...AND IYLAR FAILS TO PREVENT THE CIVIL WAR ON THE OTHER SIDE OF THE CURTAIN...
...EARTH WILL DIE!

PRESENTLY...
HAVE TO KEEP MOVING INTO THE FUTURE UNTIL I OVERTAKE IYLAR!
SHOULD BE SIMPLE ENOUGH... I DON'T NEED MY COSMIC TREADMILL SINCE I DON'T HAVE TO PINPOINT AN EXACT MOMENT IN TIME--!*
* FLASH TRAVELED INTO THE FUTURE WITHOUT THE TREADMILL IN SHOWCASE #4 (SEPT., OCT. 1956)! --JULIE

WITH EVERY OUNCE OF HIS SUPER-SPEED, FLASH RACES-- REMAINING IN THE SAME PHYSICAL SPACE, BUT MOVING FORWARD IN TIME!
THUS THE SCENE AROUND HIM SEEMS TO EVOLVE-- AS IT CHANGES WITH THE PASSAGE OF CENTURIES!...
15

WERE IT NOT FOR THE URGENCY OF HIS MISSION, FLASH MIGHT FIND THE JOURNEY PLEASANT! SOME OF THE SIGHTS RUSHING PAST HIM ARE FAMILIAR...
THOSE BUILDINGS-- I RECOGNIZE THEM! I'M PASSING THROUGH CENTRAL CITY-- IN THE 25TH CENTURY! *
* SINCE FLASH IS MOVING ONLY THROUGH TIME--NOT SPACE--HE SHOULD BE IN THE 25TH-CENTURY EQUIVALENT OF ROSEMONT... AND HE IS! IN THE FUTURE, CENTRAL CITY WILL EXPAND --BECOMING A SPRAWLING MEGALOPOLIS! --JULIE

SUDDENLY...THE MONARCH OF MOTION RUNS HEADLONG INTO SOMETHING AS FAST AS HIMSELF--IF NOT FASTER!
BWAARAM
IT WOULD HAVE TO BE--TO COLLIDE WITH FLASH BEFORE HE CAN SPEED BEYOND THIS MOMENT IN TIME...

AND BACK OVER 20TH-CENTURY EARTH...
NOW, SUPERMAN, IT IS TIME FOR YOU TO--
STAY WHERE YOU ARE, ZELKOT!
HMM...IT SEEMS YOU FORGOT THAT THE VOLKIR HAD A CREW, TOO!

THIS LOOKS LIKE WHAT MY PEOPLE CALL A "MEXICAN STANDOFF"!
INDEED--OUR LEADERS ARE UNCONSCIOUS! SINCE WE CANNOT ACT WITHOUT ORDERS, WE ARE AT AN IMPASSE!
I THINK NOT! THE ZELKOT HAVE TAKEN FLASH AS THEIR CHAMPION...
16

...SO THE VOLKIR WILL TAKE SUPERMAN AS THEIRS! THE KRYPTONIAN WILL FLY INTO THE FUTURE-- OVERTAKE THE FLASH..
...AND PREVENT THAT HATEFUL IYLAR FROM PENETRATING THE COSMIC CURTAIN!
THUS OUR GLORIOUS WAR WILL BE PRESERVED!
BUT TAKE CARE-- THE COSMIC CURTAIN CAN BE PENETRATED ONLY ONCE...
...AND THE PASSAGE CREATED BY THE FIRST MAN THROUGH IT WILL REMAIN OPEN ONLY FOR THE BRIEFEST OF TIMES!
SO... YOU MUST GET THERE FIRST!
YOU'RE KIDDING! IF YOU THINK I'D RISK GOADING THE ZELKOT INTO WIPING OUT EARTH, YOU'RE--
YOU WILL-- IF YOU VALUE YOUR OWN EXISTENCE!
YOU RECALL THAT RED-SUN PLANET THE ZELKOT COLONIZED--?
GREAT SUNS... NO!
YES! IT WAS KRYPTON! THE ZELKOT SUPPRESSED THE INTERNAL FORCES THAT WOULD HAVE DESTROYED YOUR NATIVE WORLD...
...EONS BEFORE KRYPTON EVENTUALLY DID EXPLODE!
AND IF... IF IYLAR PREVENTS THE CIVIL WAR-- THE ZELKOT WILL NEVER GO TO KRYPTON...
...KRYPTON WILL EXPLODE PREMATURELY ...AND THERE WILL NEVER BE A SUPERMAN--!
I WILL HAVE CEASED TO EXIST!!
PRECISELY.
THERE IS A LONG MOMENT IN WHICH SUPERMAN PONDERS HIS FATE-- AND THEN...
ALL RIGHT-- I'LL RUN YOUR MISERABLE ERRAND! AND IF IT MEANS EARTH MUST DIE...
...SO BE IT!
17

THAT CAN'T BE THE SUPERMAN WE KNOW... OR CAN IT?!
INTERESTING... I DID NOT THINK HE WOULD CONSENT!
NOR I! SURELY I THOUGHT HE WOULD BE WILLING TO SACRIFICE HIMSELF SO THAT EARTH MIGHT LIVE--!
AND AS FOR OUR OTHER HERO--HE IS NOT QUITE HIMSELF, EITHER! FOR HE'S NOT USED TO BEING KNOCKED SENSELESS...
YOU--! UNNH! I... I SHOULD HAVE KNOWN...
...BEING THAT I'M IN THE 25TH CENTURY... THE HOME OF...
...THE REVERSE-FLASH!
CALL ME BY MY RIGHTFUL NAME: EOBARD THAWNE--BETTER KNOWN IN "FAST COMPANY" AS...
...PROFESSOR ZOOM!
THAPETA THAPETA THAPETA THAPET
ONLY YOU REFER TO ME BY THE CONTEMPTIBLE MONIKER--"REVERSE-FLASH"...
...BUT YOU WON'T DO IT FOR LONG --NOT AFTER I TAKE ADVANTAGE OF MY INCREDIBLE GOOD LUCK--
--IN STARTING TO TRAVEL BACKWARD TOWARD YOUR CENTURY AT THE SAME TIME AS YOU WERE MOVING FORWARD INTO MINE...
...RESULTING IN THE SUPER-SPEED COLLISION THAT STUNNED YOU--
--MADE YOU WEAK AS A KITTEN!
THRAKK
YEAH--WHEN I'M FINISHED WITH YOU, I'LL BE THE FIRST AND FOREMOST FLASH...
...AND THE ONLY KIND OF FLASH YOU'LL BE...
...IS DEAD!
25 THRILL-PACKED PAGES OF STORY--
IN DC COMICS PRESENTS #2--ON SALE THE 3RD WEEK IN JUNE!
THE BIGGER WE ARE... THE BETTER WE ARE!

THE BIGGER WE ARE...
THE BETTER WE ARE!
50¢
44 PAGES ALL-NEW
NO. 2
OCT.
APPROVED BY THE COMICS CODE AUTHORITY
DC
COMICS PRESENTS
SUPERMAN AND THE FLASH
ONLY ONE OF US CAN PURSUE THAT ALIEN THROUGH THIS TIME-BARRIER, FLASH!
AND WHICHEVER ONE OF US DOESN'T MAKE IT THROUGH...
...WILL DIE!
Garcia Lopez & ADKINS
THE MAN OF STEEL AND THE SCARLET SPEEDSTER RUN A DEADLY... "RACE TO THE END OF TIME!"
25 PAGES OF PULSE-POUNDING PANDEMONIUM!
S-2942

DC COMICS PRESENTS-- TOGETHER IN ONE ADVENTURE...
SUPERMAN and THE FLASH
A FUNNY THING HAPPENED ON THE WAY TO THE FUTURE: WHILE PASSING THROUGH THE 25th CENTURY, THE FLASH COLLIDED WITH HIS OLD ENEMY PROFESSOR ZOOM! RESULT? THE SCARLET SPEEDSTER WAS KNOCKED OUT!
--AND NOW--ACCORDING TO SUPERMAN'S SUPER-HEARING AND TELESCOPIC VISION--IF ZOOM HAS HIS WAY--
--THE FLASH WILL BE KNOCKED OFF AS WELL!
THAT CAN'T BE ALLOWED TO HAPPEN--FOR THE FASTEST MAN ALIVE HAS CENTURIES TO GO AND PROMISES TO KEEP! AND IF HE BREAKS THOSE PROMISES, EARTH WILL BE DESTROYED!
BUT IF HE SUCCEEDS IN HIS MISSION, SUPERMAN WILL CEASE TO EXIST! A DOUBLY DIFFICULT DILEMMA INDEED FACES THESE TWO RELUCTANT RUNNERS IN A...
RACE TO THE END OF TIME!
HOW DID THIS RACE COME TO BE? WHERE IS THE FINISH LINE? HOLD YOUR QUESTIONS FOR NOW--BECAUSE FLASH IS IMPERILED--
-STORY- MARTIN PASKO
-ART- J.L. GARCIA LOPEZ with DAN ADKINS
-LETTERING- CLEM ROBINS
-COLORING- JERRY SERPE
-EDITING- JULIUS SCHWARTZ

--AND THAT PERIL DEMANDS OUR UNDIVIDED ATTENTION--
--AND SUPERMAN'S, AS WELL...
WHAT'S ZOOM DOING?
LOOKS LIKE HE'S STARTING TO RUN AROUND FLASH --IN A CIRCLE!
"NOW I UNDERSTAND! THE REVERSE-FLASH IS RACING FIRST IN ONE DIRECTION--THEN IN THE OTHER..."
"...BUT HE'S MOVING SO FAST..."
...IT'S AS IF HE'S GOING IN TWO OPPOSITE DIRECTIONS AT ONCE--
--SETTING UP TWO WAVES OF CONFLICTING VIBRATIONS--
--CAUSING THE FLASH TO VIBRATE IN A SIMILAR WAY...
...PULLING THE MOLECULES OF HIS BODY IN OPPOSITE DIRECTIONS --TEARING HIM APART!
I CAN'T MAKE MY PRESENCE HERE KNOWN --SO I CAN'T SWOOP DOWN TO SAVE HIM!
BUT--MAYBE A BURST OF SUPER-COLD BREATH WILL DO THE TRICK...
2

"...TO WAKE FLASH UP!"

WITHIN ONE SECOND, THE BLAST OF AIR HAS REVIVED FLASH-- AND HE HAS CORRECTLY ASSESSED THE DANGER FACING HIM!

GOT TO USE MY BODY'S VIBRATIONS...TO CRACK OPEN THE PAVEMENT UNDER ME...

...AND BURROW UNDERGROUND... SO THAT I EMERGE...

...OUTSIDE ZOOM'S DEADLY CIRCLE OF MOVEMENT!
THE FLASH-- GONE?!
CHOOM!

I PLAN TO MAKE AN IMPRESSION ON YOU FIRST! THEN I'LL BE GONE...
NO-- NOT YET, ZOOM!
...BUT NOT FORGOTTEN!
BAMM!
UNNH!

HUNH? FLASH--TAKING OFF? BUT WHY?
MAYBE HE DOESN'T REALIZE THAT PROFESSOR ZOOM IS STILL CONSCIOUS--AND "PLAYING POSSUM"!

GUESS I'LL HAVE TO RISK BEING OBSERVED BY THE ALIENS WHO ARE MONITORING US ACROSS TIME!

WHAT'S THAT? ALIENS--MONITORING FLASH AND SUPERMAN? IF THAT BAFFLES YOU, FRIENDS--HANG ON! YOU'LL GET A GLIMPSE OF THOSE ALIENS IN A PAGE OR TWO...

...BUT RIGHT NOW:

IF THE SPEEDSTER DOESN'T GET MY HELP IN NABBING THE REVERSE FLASH...

...HE MAY GET HUNG UP IN THIS TIME-PERIOD--BATTLING ZOOM--FOR WHO KNOWS HOW LONG! AND HE'LL NEVER PREVENT EARTH'S DESTRUCTION THAT WAY!

WITH A SERIES OF SUPER-SPEED KARATE CHOPS, THE CAPED KRYPTONIAN DISLODGES BLOCK AFTER BLOCK OF CONCRETE FROM THE PLAZA PAVEMENT...
MY NEXT JOB IS ROUNDING UP ZOOM AND IMPRISONING HIM HERE--
...AND AT EYE-BLURRING SPEED, HE USES THEM TO CONSTRUCT A MAKESHIFT PRISON!
--EVEN IF IT MEANS LETTING FLASH KNOW I'M HEADING INTO THE FUTURE, TOO!
4.

BUT THAT MAY NOT BE NECESSARY, SUPERMAN...
THAT SOUND--BEHIND ME! IT'S ZOOM--JUST AS I SUSPECTED...
...HE WAS LETTING ME GET A "HEAD START"--
--SO THAT HE COULD SNEAK UP BEHIND ME--
--AND CATCH ME UNAWARES!
WELL, THIS CALLS FOR ONE OF THE OLDEST TRICKS IN THE BOOK!
SO OLD, IN FACT, THAT MAYBE EVERYONE HERE IN THE 25th CENTURY HAS FORGOTTEN IT:
THE OLD FOOT-IN-THE-DOORWAY TRICK!
NO...
NO...
DON'T KNOW IF EVERYONE HAS FORGOTTEN THIS MANEUVER...
...BUT IT LOOKS LIKE ZOOM IS GOING TO FALL FOR IT...
TOO...MUCH... MOMENTUM...
CAN'T...STOP ...IN TIME--! CAN'T...ST--
...AND I DO MEAN "FALL"!
--AWP?
HAVE A NICE TRIP!
OUCH! THAT GAG WAS TOO CORNY FOR EVEN MY SENSE OF HUMOR!
NOW TO FIND SOMETHING THAT'LL PASS FOR A CELL --TO PUT THIS BOZO AWAY!
SCREEE!
WHAAMM
5

SPEAKING OF WHICH...

A CELL--?! WHERE'D IT COME FROM? IT'S LIKE SOME FAIRY GODMOTHER READ MY MIND...

...AND GRANTED MY WISH!

BUT WHO'S COMPLAINING? WITH ZOOM "ON ICE"...

...I CAN GET BACK TO WHAT I STARTED!

RUNNING IN PLACE AT SUPER-SPEED, THE FLASH VANISHES FURTHER INTO THE FUTURE!

MEANWHILE--IN A SPACECRAFT OVER 20TH-CENTURY EARTH...

OBSERVE-- IT IS THE KRYPTONIAN!

HE APPEARS TO HAVE PAUSED IN THE 25TH CENTURY...

...BUT I CANNOT BE CERTAIN!

NOR I! HE MOVES TOO QUICKLY TO BE CLEARLY SEEN--

?! LOOK, MY VOLKIR ENEMY-- LOOK AT THE SCREEN!

IT HAS GONE BLANK!

WHICH MEANS THAT THESE LIEUTENANTS OF TWO WARRING ALIEN ARMIES, WHO ARE THE ALIENS SUPERMAN WAS SO CONCERNED ABOUT-- CANNOT SEE THE CONFRONTATION BETWEEN THE TWO HEROES NOW TAKING PLACE...

SUPERMAN--!?

YOU'RE RACING INTO THE FUTURE, TOO? WHAT FOR?

TO ABORT YOUR MISSION, PAL-- THAT'S WHAT!

HUNH?! BUT WHY??

BECAUSE JUST AS THE ZELKOT HAVE MADE YOU THEIR PAWN--I'M THE VOLKIR'S CHAMPION...

...AND FROM HERE ON IN, WE'RE ENEMIES!

B-BUT I'M DOING THIS FOR EARTH'S BENEFIT--NOT THE ZELKOT'S!

FOR A BRIEF MOMENT, SUPERMAN STUDIES FLASH'S FACE...

6

...AND SEES MIRRORED THERE HIS OWN RAGE AND FRUSTRATION! "HOW CAN THIS BE HAPPENING?" THEY ASK THEMSELVES! BUT BOTH MEN KNOW HOW:
THEY HAD COME TO A SMALL TOWN--TO SAVE IT FROM BEING DESTROYED BY A STRANGE BEAM FROM OUTER SPACE!
IN TRACKING THE BEAM TO ITS SOURCE HIGH OVER EARTH, THEY WERE CAPTURED-- AND IMPRISONED IN A NEUTRAL TERRITORY FORMED BY THE JOINING OF TWO SPACECRAFT! THERE THEY LEARNED THE STORY OF THEIR CAPTORS...
...MEMBERS OF TWO ALIEN RACES-- THE ZELKOT AND THE VOLKIR--WHO HAD BEEN AT WAR FOR COUNTLESS MILLENNIA!
THE ZELKOT AND THE VOLKIR WERE DESCENDED FROM COMMON ANCESTORS--AND BILLIONS OF YEARS AGO, THE PARENT-RACE ROAMED THE UNIVERSE, SETTLING ON MANY PLANETS! THEY CAME TO EARTH IN THE DAWN OF ITS TIME--AND LIVED DURING ITS PRE-HISTORY FOR MANY EONS...
BUT THERE CAME A STRIFE AMONG THEM--A CIVIL WAR THAT SPLIT THE ANCESTOR RACE INTO TWO FACTIONS! THEY LEFT EARTH--EACH GROUP GOING ITS OWN WAY...
...AND DOWN THROUGH THE CENTURIES, EACH GROUP EVOLVED--UNTIL THERE WERE TWO SEPARATE RACES-- THE ZELKOT AND THE VOLKIR!
7.

BUT EVOLUTION HAD TAKEN ITS COURSE ON ALL THE WORLDS THE ALIENS HAD VISITED, TOO! THEIR SPACECRAFT WERE LIVING CREATURES-- AND IN THE WASTE MATTER THE LIVING SHIPS LEFT BEHIND WERE MICROSCOPIC ORGANISMS WHICH EVOLVED INTO HUMANOID LIFE!
IN THAT WAY, THE ANCESTOR RACE PLANTED LIFE ALL OVER THE UNIVERSE...ON EARTH AND ON A PLANET IN A RED-SUN SYSTEM VISITED BY THE FACTION THAT LATER BECAME THE VOLKIR!
THE VOLKIR LIVED ON THAT PLANET FOR A TIME-- AFTER USING THEIR TECHNOLOGY TO STOP THE INTERNAL PRESSURES THAT WOULD HAVE CAUSED THE PLANET TO EXPLODE!
WHEN THE TWO RACES MET IN SPACE YEARS LATER, THEY RESUMED THEIR WAR...
...AND SO IT WAS, THROUGHOUT THE MILLENNIA, UNTIL THE ZELKOT--WEARY OF A WAR WHOSE CAUSE THEY NO LONGER REMEMBERED--DECIDED TO END THE WAR...
...BY SENDING AN AGENT NAMED IYLAR THROUGH TIME--TO THE POINT IN EARTH'S PREHISTORY WHEN THE ANCESTOR RACE'S CIVIL WAR BEGAN--TO PREVENT IT! HOWEVER...
...THE WARLIKE VOLKIR WANT THE WAR TO CONTINUE--AND THEY'VE SOMEHOW PLANTED BOOBY TRAPS ALONG THE PATH--TO STOP IYLAR!
IF I DON'T HELP HIM GET PAST THE TRAPS, THE ZELKOT WILL DESTROY EARTH WITH THE BEAM THE VOLKIR USED ON THAT TOWN...
...IN HOPES OF KILLING IYLAR BEFORE HE COULD MOVE THROUGH TIME!
SO WHY WOULD SUPERMAN RISK EARTH'S DESTRUCTION BY OPPOSING FLASH? HE OFFERS NO ANSWER... HE MERELY CONTINUES INTO THE FUTURE-- IN SILENCE...
8.

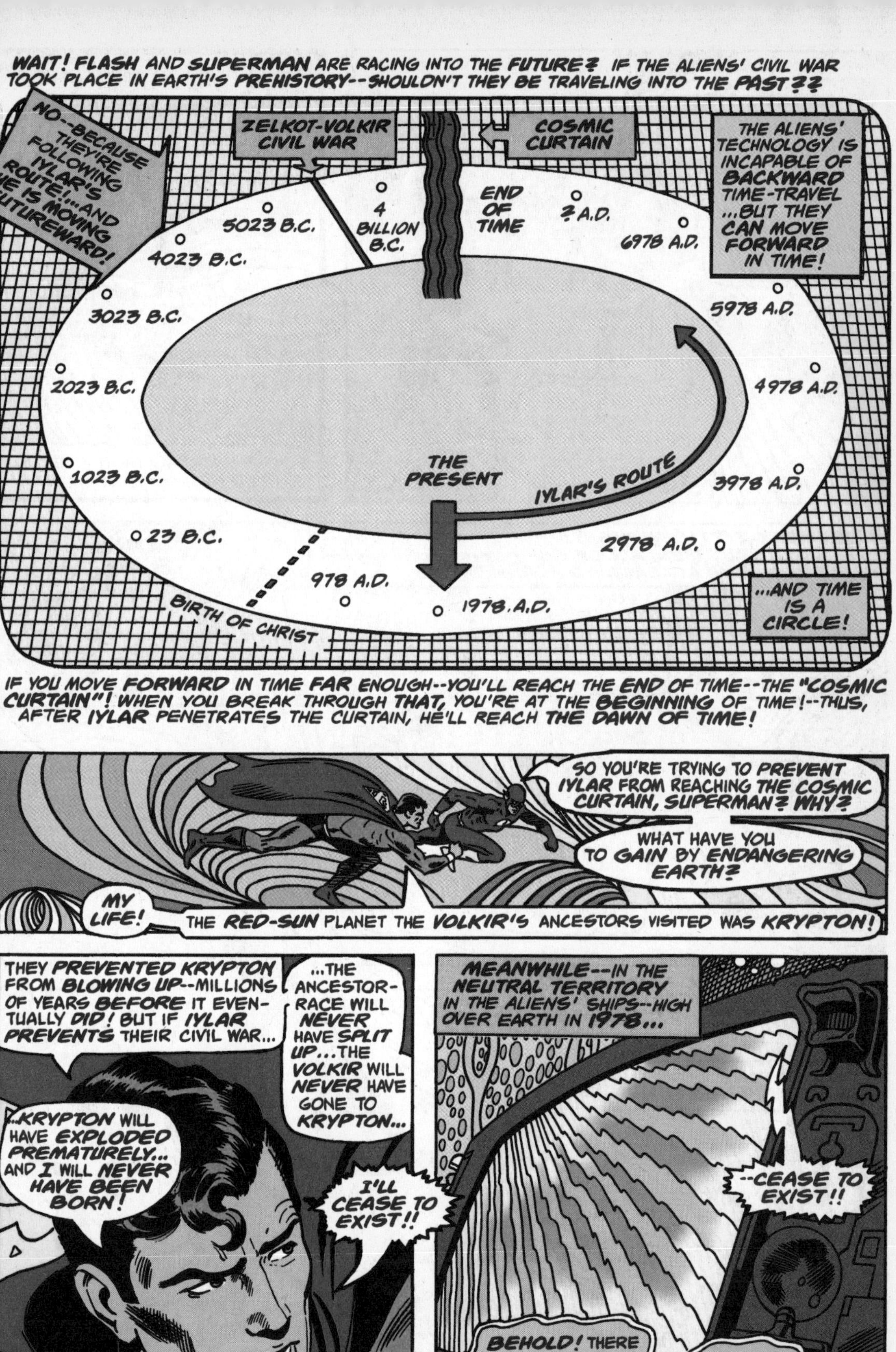
WAIT! FLASH AND SUPERMAN ARE RACING INTO THE FUTURE? IF THE ALIENS' CIVIL WAR TOOK PLACE IN EARTH'S PREHISTORY--SHOULDN'T THEY BE TRAVELING INTO THE PAST??
NO--BECAUSE THEY'RE FOLLOWING IYLAR'S ROUTE!...AND HE IS MOVING FUTUREWARD!
ZELKOT-VOLKIR CIVIL WAR
COSMIC CURTAIN
THE ALIENS' TECHNOLOGY IS INCAPABLE OF BACKWARD TIME-TRAVEL ...BUT THEY CAN MOVE FORWARD IN TIME!
5023 B.C.
4 BILLION B.C.
END OF TIME
? A.D.
6978 A.D.
4023 B.C.
3023 B.C.
5978 A.D.
2023 B.C.
4978 A.D.
1023 B.C.
THE PRESENT
IYLAR'S ROUTE
3978 A.D.
23 B.C.
2978 A.D.
978 A.D.
1978 A.D.
BIRTH OF CHRIST
...AND TIME IS A CIRCLE!
IF YOU MOVE FORWARD IN TIME FAR ENOUGH--YOU'LL REACH THE END OF TIME--THE "COSMIC CURTAIN"! WHEN YOU BREAK THROUGH THAT, YOU'RE AT THE BEGINNING OF TIME!--THUS, AFTER IYLAR PENETRATES THE CURTAIN, HE'LL REACH THE DAWN OF TIME!
SO YOU'RE TRYING TO PREVENT IYLAR FROM REACHING THE COSMIC CURTAIN, SUPERMAN? WHY?
WHAT HAVE YOU TO GAIN BY ENDANGERING EARTH?
MY LIFE!
THE RED-SUN PLANET THE VOLKIR'S ANCESTORS VISITED WAS KRYPTON!
THEY PREVENTED KRYPTON FROM BLOWING UP--MILLIONS OF YEARS BEFORE IT EVENTUALLY DID! BUT IF IYLAR PREVENTS THEIR CIVIL WAR...
...THE ANCESTOR-RACE WILL NEVER HAVE SPLIT UP...THE VOLKIR WILL NEVER HAVE GONE TO KRYPTON...
...KRYPTON WILL HAVE EXPLODED PREMATURELY... AND I WILL NEVER HAVE BEEN BORN!
I'LL CEASE TO EXIST!!
MEANWHILE--IN THE NEUTRAL TERRITORY IN THE ALIENS' SHIPS--HIGH OVER EARTH IN 1978...
--CEASE TO EXIST!!
BEHOLD! THERE IS NO LONGER AN IMAGE ON THE MONITOR...
...BUT WE STILL HAVE SOUND!
9

IT MUST BE A MALFUNCTION OF THE COMMUNICATOR-BRACELETS WITH WHICH WE EQUIPPED OUR CHAMPIONS!
THEY TRANSMIT AN IMAGE WHEN THE SO-CALLED SUPERHEROES PAUSE IN A SPECIFIC TIME-PERIOD...
...BUT NOT WHEN THEY ARE MOVING THROUGH THE INTERDIMENSIONAL LIMBO BETWEEN UNITS OF TIME!
AYE! WHEN THEY MOVE THROUGH THE NEBULOUS SPACE WE CALL THE TIME-STREAM, THEY CANNOT BE SEEN...
...BUT WE CAN HEAR THEM!
AND THE COMMUNICATION IS TWO-WAY!
GOOD! KNOWING WHAT I'VE JUST LEARNED WILL COME IN HANDY!
THOSE ARE CRYPTIC THOUGHTS THE MAN OF STEEL IS THINKING--BUT THEN, ALL OF SUPERMAN'S BEHAVIOR IS STRANGE NOW! AT LEAST, SO FLASH THINKS...
I DON'T BELIEVE IT--SUPERMAN RISKING EARTH JUST TO SAVE HIS OWN LOUSY SKIN!
HE'S A HERO, BLAST IT--HE SHOULD BE WILLING TO SACRIFICE HIMSELF SO--
--EH? THERE'S IYLAR AHEAD!
BUT WHAT'S SUPERMAN DOING? FLYING COUNTER-CLOCKWISE AT SUPER-SPEED?
OF COURSE...
"...THAT'S HOW HE TRAVELS INTO THE FUTURE--INSTANTANEOUSLY! HE'S TRYING TO OVERTAKE ME!"
BUT BEFORE EITHER HERO CAN REACH IYLAR...
BADOOM!
...AN EXPLOSION ROCKS THE ZELKOT'S TIME-SCOOTER...
10

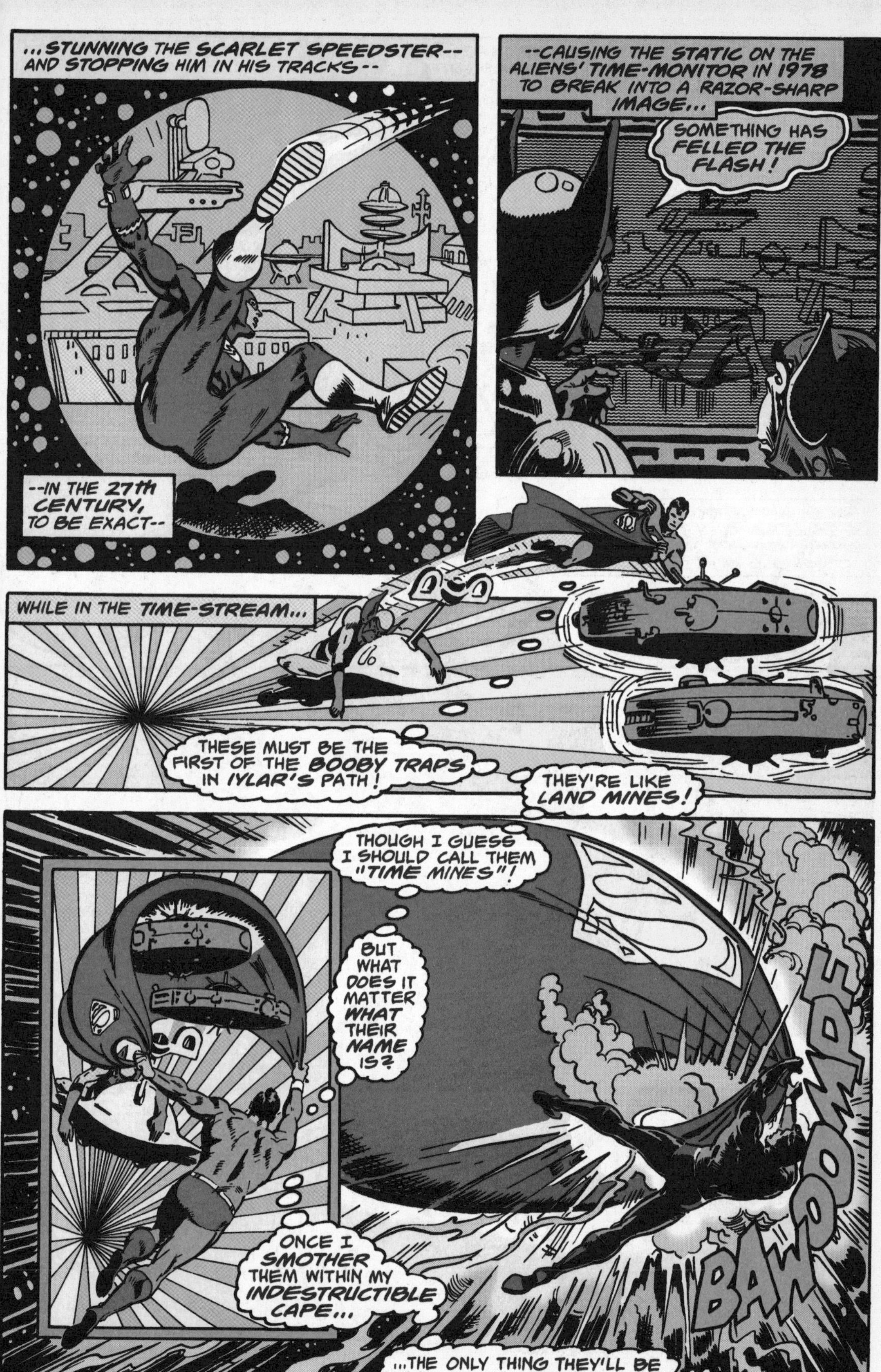
...STUNNING THE SCARLET SPEEDSTER-- AND STOPPING HIM IN HIS TRACKS--
--IN THE 27th CENTURY, TO BE EXACT--
--CAUSING THE STATIC ON THE ALIENS' TIME-MONITOR IN 1978 TO BREAK INTO A RAZOR-SHARP IMAGE...
SOMETHING HAS FELLED THE FLASH!
WHILE IN THE TIME-STREAM...
THESE MUST BE THE FIRST OF THE BOOBY TRAPS IN IYLAR'S PATH!
THEY'RE LIKE LAND MINES!
THOUGH I GUESS I SHOULD CALL THEM "TIME MINES"!
BUT WHAT DOES IT MATTER WHAT THEIR NAME IS?
ONCE I SMOTHER THEM WITHIN MY INDESTRUCTIBLE CAPE...
...THE ONLY THING THEY'LL BE CALLED IS HARMLESS!
BAWOOOMPF
11.

UNNH! YOU--
SPEEDING STRANGER...
...WHO...ARE YOU? I HAVE NOT SEEN YOUR LIKE BEFORE--!
THAT IS IYLAR'S VOICE!
BUT WHAT IS HAPPENING?
CAN YOU NOT TELL, ZELKOT SWINE?
SINCE THE FLASH LIES STRICKEN IN THE 27th CENTURY...
...IT MEANS OUR CHAMPION--SUPERMAN--IS ATTACKING IYLAR!
"--WHICH MEANS, TOO, THAT WE WILL BE SUCCESSFUL IN THWARTING YOUR HATEFUL ATTEMPT TO END OUR GLORIOUS WAR!"
IT CERTAINLY DOES SEEM AS IF SUPERMAN IS WORKING FOR THE VOLKIR, DOESN'T IT? BUT...
I HATE DOING THIS--WISH I COULD EXPLAIN THINGS TO IYLAR...
...BUT I HAVE TO KEEP QUIET --OR THE ALIENS WOULD OVERHEAR --AND KNOW I'M NOT ABOUT TO HELP EITHER OF THEM!
SPEEDING STRANGER--WHY DO YOU--ARRGH!
SO, ZELKOT--IT SEEMS SUPERMAN IS THE VICTOR! BUT WITHOUT SEEING--HOW MAY WE BE CERTAIN?
YOU CANNOT, VOLKIR CUR! THERE IS YET HOPE FOR THE ZELKOT CAUSE!
12.

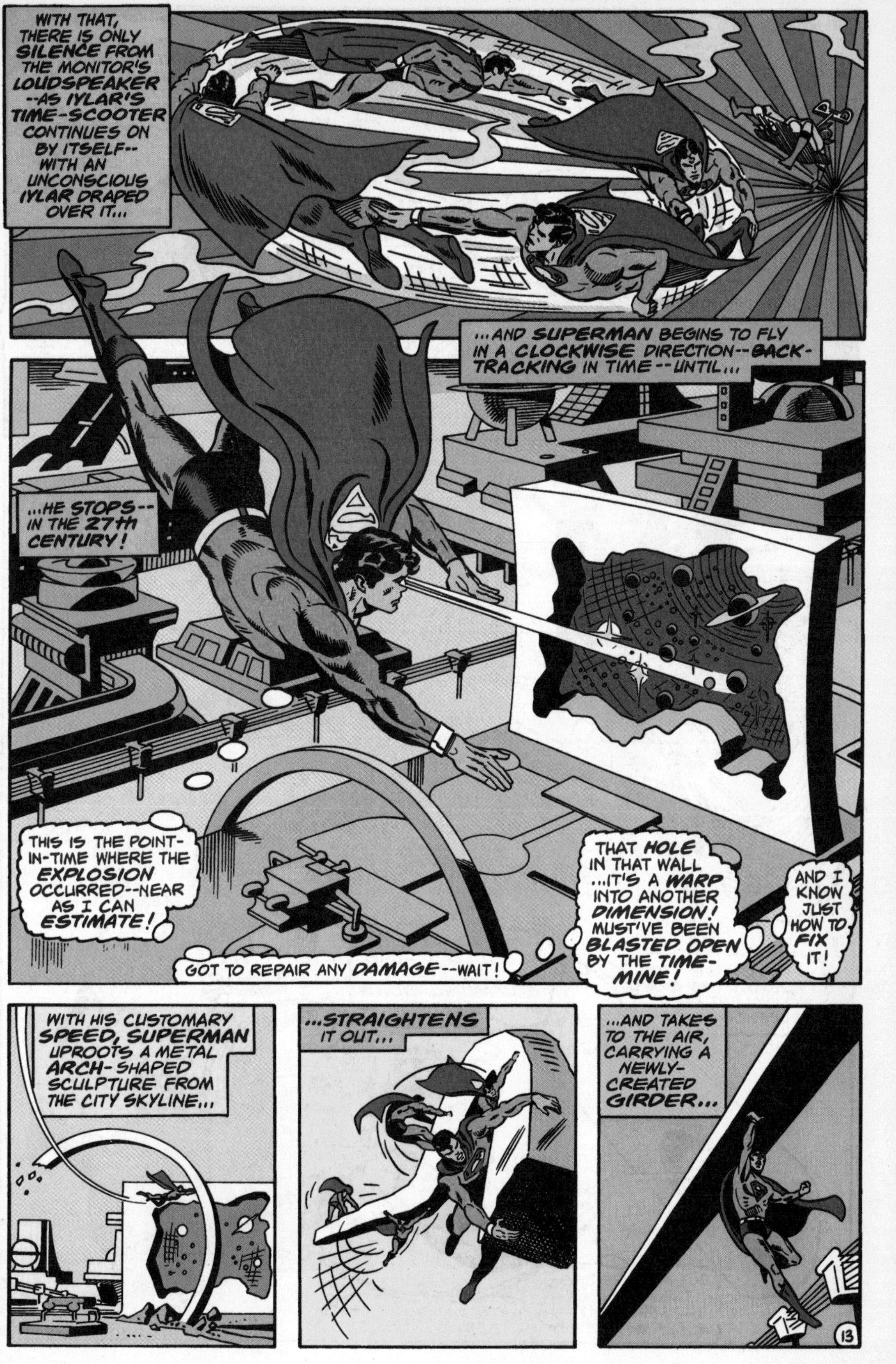

WITH THAT, THERE IS ONLY SILENCE FROM THE MONITOR'S LOUDSPEAKER --AS IYLAR'S TIME-SCOOTER CONTINUES ON BY ITSELF-- WITH AN UNCONSCIOUS IYLAR DRAPED OVER IT...

...AND SUPERMAN BEGINS TO FLY IN A CLOCKWISE DIRECTION--BACK-TRACKING IN TIME--UNTIL...

...HE STOPS-- IN THE 27th CENTURY!

THIS IS THE POINT-IN-TIME WHERE THE EXPLOSION OCCURRED--NEAR AS I CAN ESTIMATE!

GOT TO REPAIR ANY DAMAGE--WAIT!

THAT HOLE IN THAT WALL ...IT'S A WARP INTO ANOTHER DIMENSION! MUST'VE BEEN BLASTED OPEN BY THE TIME-MINE!

AND I KNOW JUST HOW TO FIX IT!

WITH HIS CUSTOMARY SPEED, SUPERMAN UPROOTS A METAL ARCH-SHAPED SCULPTURE FROM THE CITY SKYLINE...

...STRAIGHTENS IT OUT...

...AND TAKES TO THE AIR, CARRYING A NEWLY-CREATED GIRDER...
13

THE HOLE IN THAT WALL IS DANGER-OUS--
PEOPLE AND THINGS FROM THIS DIMENSION COULD BE LOST BY ACCIDENTALLY FALLING THROUGH IT!
AND WHO KNOWS WHAT HORRORS EXIST IN THE OTHER DIMENSION...
...OR WHAT COULD ENTER THROUGH THE WARP?
IN ORDER TO CLOSE IT, I'LL NEED THIS CABLE!

WITH THAT, HE PUNCHES A HOLE IN ONE END OF HIS NEWLY-FASHIONED "GIRDER"...

...AND WITH SUPER-STRENGTH, HE STREAMLINES IT--SHARPENING THE OTHER END INTO A FINE POINT!

THE RESULT: A GIGANTIC IMPROVISED NEEDLE--WHOSE THREAD IS...

...THIS CABLE--IT'S PROBABLY THIS ERA'S EQUIVALENT OF A TELEPHONE LINE--

--AND BORROWING IT COULD DISTURB THE FLOW OF COMMUNICATIONS IN THIS CENTURY!

BUT CONSIDERING THE POSSIBLY UNPLEASANT ALTERNATIVE--

--IT'S A RISK THAT MUST BE TAKEN!

14

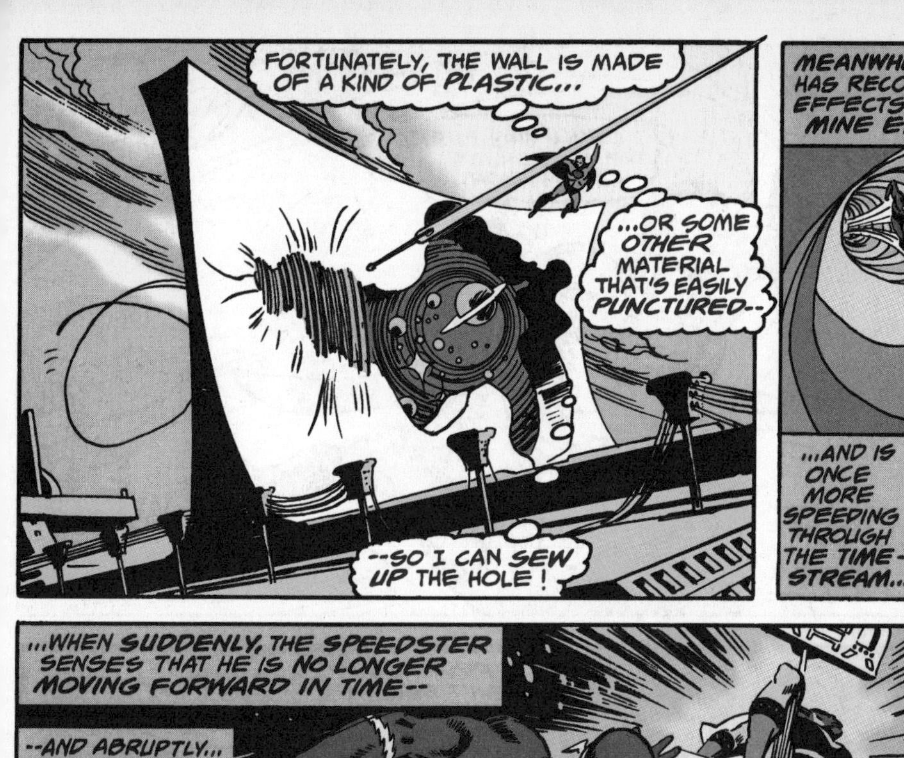

FORTUNATELY, THE WALL IS MADE OF A KIND OF PLASTIC...
...OR SOME OTHER MATERIAL THAT'S EASILY PUNCTURED--
--SO I CAN SEW UP THE HOLE!

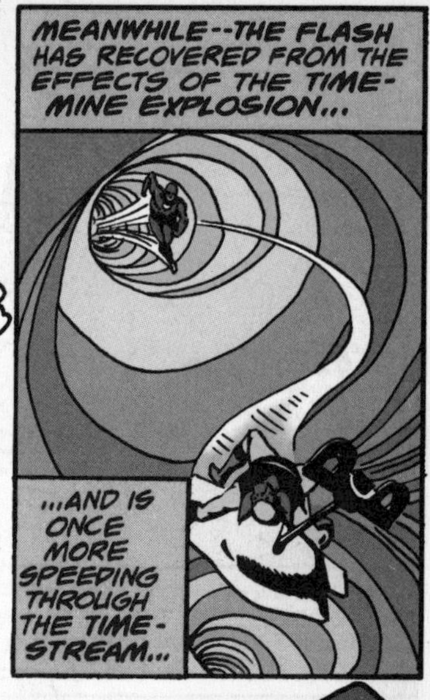

MEANWHILE--THE FLASH HAS RECOVERED FROM THE EFFECTS OF THE TIME-MINE EXPLOSION...
...AND IS ONCE MORE SPEEDING THROUGH THE TIME-STREAM...

...WHEN SUDDENLY, THE SPEEDSTER SENSES THAT HE IS NO LONGER MOVING FORWARD IN TIME--

--AND ABRUPTLY... INEXPLICABLY... EVERYTHING AROUND HIM... GOES BLACK!

WHUMP

I'M IN TOTAL DARKNESS--CAN'T SEE!

BUT THAT NOISE--IT SOUNDS LIKE IYLAR'S COLLIDED WITH SOME KIND OF OBSTACLE!

HE CAN'T MOVE, EITHER!

...WHICH MEANS WE'RE PROBABLY... TRAPPED INSIDE SOMETHING!!

15.

MEANWHILE...
THERE--IT'S FINISHED!
I COULD HAVE FUSED THE HOLE SHUT WITH MY HEAT-VISION...
...BUT IT MIGHT HAVE OPENED UP AGAIN AFTER THE MATERIAL COOLED! THIS WAY THE SEAL IS PERMANENT!

I'D BETTER GET A MOVE ON!
FLASH HAS PROBABLY GAINED A CONSIDERABLE ADVANTAGE BY NOW!!
BUT PROGRESS DOESN'T SEEM TO BE IN THE CARDS FOR EITHER OF OUR STALWARTS THIS DAY...
--EH? BLUE SKY--CLOUDS--?
THAT MEANS I'M NOT ADVANCING THROUGH TIME ANY-MORE!
I'M STILL AIRBORNE--BUT I'M STUCK IN THIS TIME-PERIOD... WHENEVER "THIS" IS!

AS FOR THE FLASH--HE, TOO, IS MYSTIFIED BY HIS OWN WHEREABOUTS...

WE'RE INSIDE A CYLINDRICAL DWELLING OF SOME SORT--! IT MUST'VE BEEN BUILT IN THE EXACT SPOT I WAS RUNNING IN!

SO WHEN WE ENTERED THIS TIME-PERIOD, IT "SPRANG UP" AROUND US--EH?

SOMETHING WRITTEN ON IYLAR'S TUNIC--?

trust me. Superman

A MESSAGE...FROM SUPERMAN--? WELL, I'LL BE--!

GUESS I SHOULD'VE KNOWN BETTER THAN TO THINK HE'D COP OUT ON EARTH!

I DON'T KNOW WHAT HIS PLAN IS...

...BUT I MUST ADMIT I'M RELIEVED!

16

WITH THAT WORRY TAKEN CARE OF...
...I'LL DEAL WITH GETTING OUT OF HERE...
...BY VIBRATING MY BODY...
...AS I PUSH AGAINST THE WALL OF THIS STRUCTURE!
...IT SHOULD START VIBRATING, TOO...
...AND EVENTUALLY --CRACK APART!
CHOOM!
THERE--WE'RE OUT OF THE FRYING PAN...
...I JUST HOPE WE HAVEN'T JUMPED INTO A FIRE--
WHOOPS!
FUNNY I SHOULD THINK THAT!
THERE GOES IYLAR, I SEE--ON "AUTOMATIC PILOT" INTO THE FUTURE! GUESS HE DIDN'T FEEL LIKE STICKING AROUND TO MEET THE "NATIVES"!
WELL, ONE THING'S FAIRLY CLEAR...
...A WELCOME WAGON IT ISN'T!
ELSEWHERE IN TIME:
WAIT--THAT BUILDING DOWN THERE--
--IT'S THE HEAD-QUARTERS OF...
..."THE LEGION OF SUPER-HEROES!"
17.

NOW I THINK I KNOW WHY I'M STUCK HERE--!
HELLO, GROUP-- I NEED YOUR HELP!
SUPERMAN!
WHAT ARE YOU DOING IN THIS TIME-PERIOD?
GOOD QUESTION-- IF YOU REALLY ARE SUPERMAN...
...WHICH IS DOUBTFUL-- CONSIDERING THAT I'M SUPERBOY... YOUR YOUNGER SELF!
AMAZING! THEN MY THEORY IS CORRECT--!
WE WISH WE COULD STAY TO HEAR IT--
AFTER ALL, IT'S NOT EVERY DAY YOU HEAR A PERFECTLY SANE PERSON TALKING TO HIMSELF...
...BUT RIGHT NOW, WE'RE WORRIED ABOUT THE FLASH--
KCHOK!
DON'T KNOW WHAT THESE CREATURES ARE--OR WHY THEY'RE HOSTILE...
...BUT IT DOESN'T CHANGE THE FACT THAT I'VE GOT TO GET OUT OF HERE...
...BECAUSE NO MATTER WHAT CENTURY THIS IS --A SHARP SPEARHEAD IS STILL A SHA-- ARRGHH!
WHILE IN THE 30th CENTURY...
OKAY, FELLAS...
IF YOU THINK BANGING YOUR HEADS TOGETHER IS GOING TO SOLVE YOUR PROBLEM-- SWELL!
PERSONALLY, I THINK YOU'VE BOTH BANGED YOUR HEADS ONE TIME TOO MANY--
--BUT THAT'S YOUR PROBLEM! ON YOUR MARKS...

GET SET...
THE SIGNAL TRANSMITTED ACROSS TIME BY THE ALIEN COMMUNICATOR I'M WEARING DID THIS--
--DISTURBED THE SPACE-TIME CONTINUUM--DISTORTING THE NATURAL LAWS--ALLOWING ME TO CO-EXIST WITH A VERSION OF MYSELF FROM AN EARLIER TIME OF MY LIFE!
BUT AS A RESULT OF THE DISRUPTION, BOTH SUPERBOY AND I ARE TRAPPED HERE IN THE 30th CENTURY!

I ONCE DREAMED ABOUT A SITUATION LIKE THIS--WHEN I WAS SUPERBOY!*
AND IN THAT DREAM, WE SOLVED OUR PROBLEM WITH A DELIBERATE HEAD-ON COLLISION BETWEEN US!
GO!
*SHOWN IN SUPER-TEAM FAMILY #5 (JULY, 1976).--JULIE.

"THE IMPACT OF AN IRRESISTIBLE FORCE MEETING AN IMMOVABLE OBJECT--NAMELY, THE TWO OF US--HURLED US BACK TO OUR RESPECTIVE TIMES!"
BARAMMM
"I JUST HOPE IT WORKS IN REAL LIFE, TOO!"

IT DOES INDEED--FOR AS SUPERBOY IS PROPELLED BACKWARD IN TIME TO HIS OWN ERA--IN SMALLVILLE--
WELCOME to SMALLVILLE

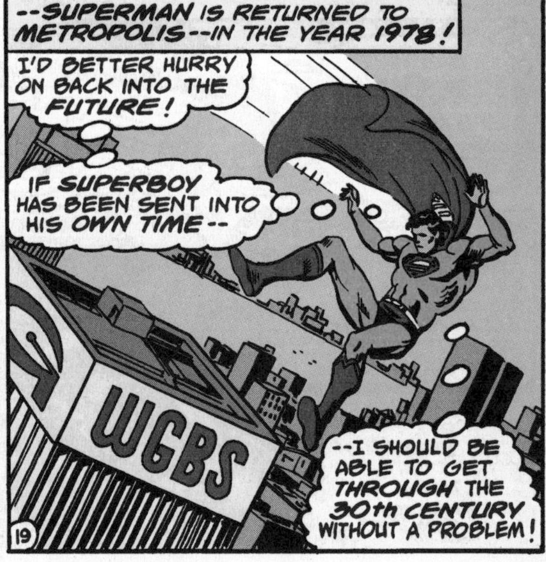
--SUPERMAN IS RETURNED TO METROPOLIS--IN THE YEAR 1978!
I'D BETTER HURRY ON BACK INTO THE FUTURE!
IF SUPERBOY HAS BEEN SENT INTO HIS OWN TIME--
--I SHOULD BE ABLE TO GET THROUGH THE 30th CENTURY WITHOUT A PROBLEM!
WGBS
19

MEANWHILE...
OBSERVE-- NOT ONLY IS THE IMAGE RELAYED BY THE COMMUNICATOR-BRACELETS GONE...
...BUT ALL AUDIO TRANSMISSION HAS NOW CEASED AS WELL!
WHY SHOULD THAT BE? WE'LL LEARN THE ANSWER MOMENTARILY...

...BUT LET US FIRST REJOIN THE FLASH, WHO IS-- SURPRISINGLY--QUITE UNHARMED...
DON'T KNOW WHY THAT CREATURE'S SPEAR DIDN'T HURT ME...
BUT I WON'T ARGUE THE POINT!

SPEEDING BACK INTO THE TIME-STREAM, HE DISCOVERS...
SO THAT'S IT! THE SPEAR STRUCK MY WRIST--BUT SHATTERED MY COMMUNICATOR INSTEAD OF WOUNDING ME!
MINE'S BEEN DESTROYED, TOO!
--WHEN I COLLIDED WITH SUPERBOY!

SUPERMAN!
I COULDN'T EXPLAIN THINGS EARLIER, FLASH--
--BECAUSE THE ALIENS MIGHT HAVE HEARD!

SO I ETCHED THAT MESSAGE INTO THE METALLIC FABRIC OF IYLAR'S TUNIC WITH MY SUPER-HARD THUMB-NAIL!
THE ALIEN COMMUNICATED WITH US TELEPATHICALLY WHEN WE FIRST ENCOUNTERED THEM--AND I'M SURE THE BRACELETS INSTANTLY TRANSLATED ALL SPEECH THEY PICKED UP INTO THEIR LANGUAGE!
SO THE MESSAGE WAS A GOOD RISK--I WAS BETTING THAT EVEN IF THE ALIENS SAW IT, THEY COULDN'T READ ENGLISH!
I AGREED TO "WORK FOR" THE VOLKIR BECAUSE I COULDN'T ALLOW THE WAR TO BE "PHASED OUT" OF EXISTENCE--OR EARTH MIGHT HAVE BEEN, TOO!
IT WAS THEIR SHIPS' EXHAUST THAT STARTED LIFE ON EARTH! AND THEY CAME HERE DURING THE WAR!
SOON, THE VERY LAND BENEATH THEIR FEET BREAKS UP INTO SMALL FLOATING CHUNKS AS THEY MOVE FORWARD IN TIME--
--FOR THIS IS ALL THAT IS LEFT OF EARTH IN THE DISTANT FUTURE...
LOOK--UP AHEAD...
...THAT MUST BE IT...
20

...THE COSMIC CURTAIN!
AND IYLAR'S ABOUT TO BREAK THROUGH IT!
WE'VE GOT TO HURRY-- OVERTAKE HIM!
"TOO LATE--HE'S PENETRATED THE CURTAIN!"
AND ACCORDING TO THE ALIENS...
...THERE'S ONLY ROOM ENOUGH FOR ONE PERSON TO SLIP THROUGH THE OPENING TORN IN THE CURTAIN! IT CAN ONLY BE PENETRATED ONCE!
AND NOW THE HOLE'S CLOSING BY ITSELF! WE'VE MISSED OUR CHANCE!*
NOT YET...
*ALL AS PREDICTED LAST ISSUE! --JULIE
I HAVE AN IDEA! YOU GO AHEAD THROUGH THE HOLE, FLASH...
...BUT VIBRATE AS YOU RUN...
...OF COURSE!
21

BY VIBRATING AS I GO THROUGH, I MAKE THE MOLECULES OF MY BODY DIFFUSE!
EXACTLY-- SO I CAN FLY THROUGH YOUR BODY AS YOU GO THROUGH THE HOLE--
...ALLOWING US BOTH TO PASS OVER TO THE OTHER SIDE OF THE CURTAIN SIMULTANEOUSLY!
THUS, AT THE DAWN OF TIME...
QUICKLY, FLASH--TAKE IYLAR BY SURPRISE WHILE I SNATCH HIS TIME-SCOOTER!
THE ZELKOT ARE PRIMARILY A PEACEFUL RACE--THEY AREN'T USED TO FISTICUFFS! YOU SHOULD BE ABLE TO KAYO HIM WITH THE OLD ONE-TWO!
THAT FELLOW HAS A GLASS JAW IF I EVER FELT ONE!
A BURST OF CONCENTRATED HEAT VISION...
...AND THIS TIME-SCOOTER IS READY FOR THE SLAG-HEAP!
NOW THAT WE'VE MADE SURE IYLAR CAN'T ESCAPE FROM US--LET'S GET OUT OF HERE!
22

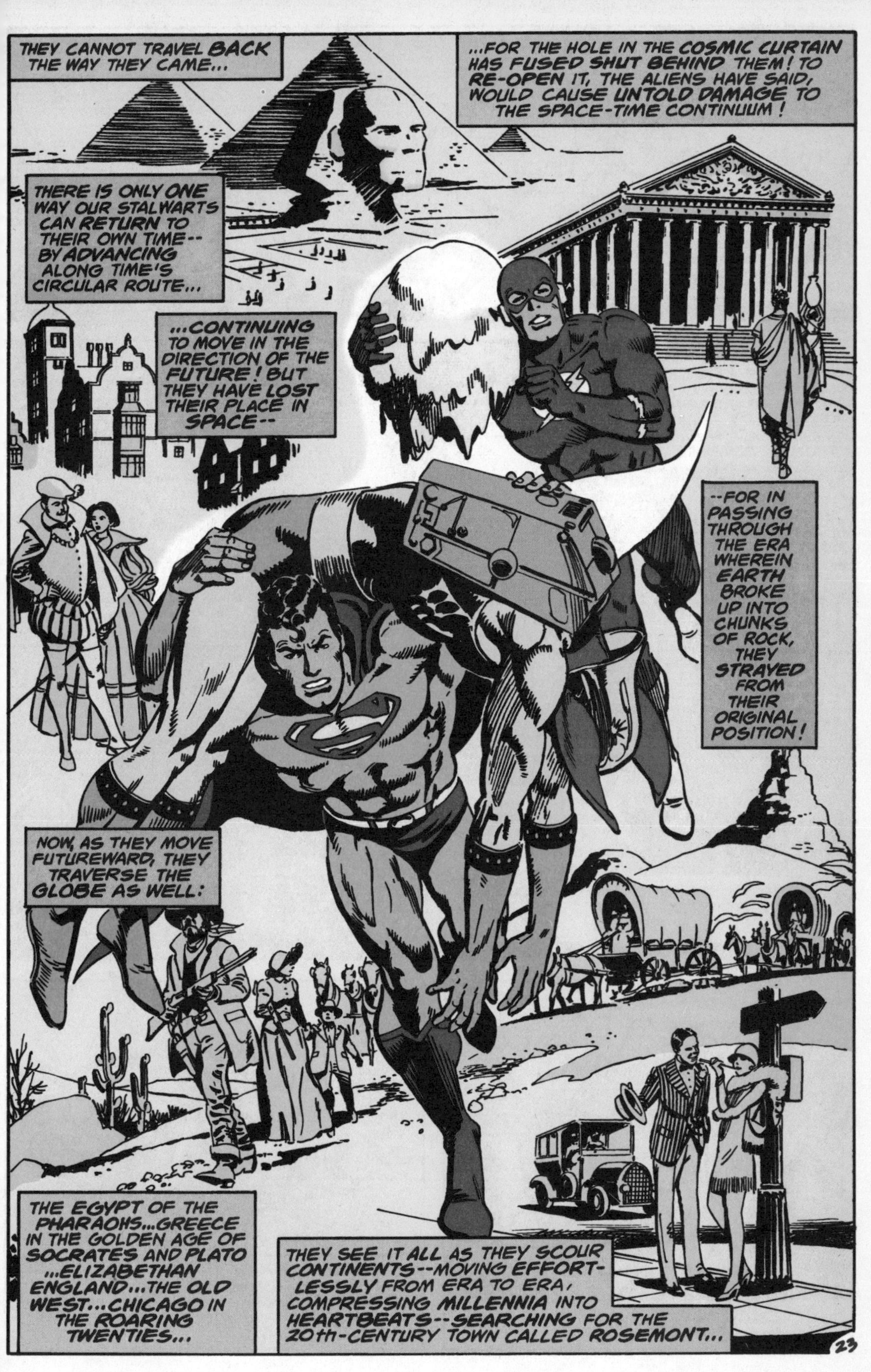
THEY CANNOT TRAVEL BACK THE WAY THEY CAME...
...FOR THE HOLE IN THE COSMIC CURTAIN HAS FUSED SHUT BEHIND THEM! TO RE-OPEN IT, THE ALIENS HAVE SAID, WOULD CAUSE UNTOLD DAMAGE TO THE SPACE-TIME CONTINUUM!
THERE IS ONLY ONE WAY OUR STALWARTS CAN RETURN TO THEIR OWN TIME-- BY ADVANCING ALONG TIME'S CIRCULAR ROUTE...
...CONTINUING TO MOVE IN THE DIRECTION OF THE FUTURE! BUT THEY HAVE LOST THEIR PLACE IN SPACE--
--FOR IN PASSING THROUGH THE ERA WHEREIN EARTH BROKE UP INTO CHUNKS OF ROCK, THEY STRAYED FROM THEIR ORIGINAL POSITION!
NOW, AS THEY MOVE FUTUREWARD, THEY TRAVERSE THE GLOBE AS WELL:
THE EGYPT OF THE PHARAOHS...GREECE IN THE GOLDEN AGE OF SOCRATES AND PLATO ...ELIZABETHAN ENGLAND...THE OLD WEST...CHICAGO IN THE ROARING TWENTIES...
THEY SEE IT ALL AS THEY SCOUR CONTINENTS--MOVING EFFORTLESSLY FROM ERA TO ERA, COMPRESSING MILLENNIA INTO HEARTBEATS--SEARCHING FOR THE 20th-CENTURY TOWN CALLED ROSEMONT...
23

UNTIL...
FINALLY-- WE MADE IT! ROSEMONT-- ON TUESDAY, JUNE 20, 1978!
OUR JOB'S NOT FINISHED YET, THOUGH!
YOU ARE NOW ENTERING ROSEMONT POP.: 575
I'LL WRAP YOU AND IYLAR IN MY CAPE--TO PROTECT YOU FROM THE COLD OF SPACE! WE'LL GET WHERE WE'RE GOING AT SUPER-SPEED-- BEFORE YOU CAN SUFFOCATE IN THE VACUUM!

TOGETHER, THEY FORM A PLAN OF ATTACK-- AND SECONDS LATER, THEY ARE SOARING SPACEWARD TOWARD THE TWO ALIEN SHIPS DOCKED IN SPACE...
THESE LIVING SHIPS ARE OBVIOUSLY "BRED" TO WITHSTAND THE FREEZING COLD OF SPACE...
...BUT I'M BETTING THEY CAN'T STAND UP TO MY SUPER-COLD BREATH...

THE FLASH'S HAND MOVES QUICKER THAN THE EYE CAN FOLLOW...
SNAP!
...AND BREAKS OFF THE LEVER THAT CONTROLS THE ZELKOT'S VIBRATIONAL BEAM...
VIBRATIONAL BEAM CONTROL
THERE--NOW THE ZELKOT COULDN'T CAUSE EARTH TO VIBRATE INTO ANOTHER DIMENSION--AS THEY THREATENED--
--EVEN IF THEY WERE CONSCIOUS ENOUGH TO TRY!
RIGHT--ACCORDING TO MY X-RAY VISION, THERE ISN'T A SINGLE ALIEN ON EITHER SHIP WHO HASN'T BEEN KNOCKED OUT!
A HANDFUL OF SECONDS LATER, AFTER RETURNING HIS SPEEDY COMPATRIOT TO EARTH...
A SUPER-STRONG TOSS--AND WHEN THE ZELKOT AND VOLKIR COME TO, THEY'LL BE AT THE OTHER END OF THE GALAXY!
LET THEM DUKE IT OUT THERE! THEY WON'T RETURN TO THIS SPACE-SECTOR--NOT WITH FLASH AND ME ON THE LOOKOUT FOR THEM!
AND SO... BACK IN ROSEMONT...
CONGRATULATIONS, PARTNER--ON PULLING A SPECTACULAR VICTORY OUT OF A NO-WIN SITUATION!
METROPOLIS 322 MI.
CENTRAL CITY 102 MI.
COME ON BACK TO MY PLACE IN CENTRAL CITY, SUPERMAN!
I'LL PUT ON SOME COFFEE...AND WE CAN RELAX A WHILE!
SURE--WHY NOT? NOW, I HAVE ALL THE TIME IN THE WORLD!
NEXT: WHAT HAPPENS WHEN EARTH SWITCHES PLACES IN SPACE --WITH AN ALIEN WORLD? SUPERMAN AND ADAM STRANGE TACKLE THE... "RIDDLE OF LITTLE PLANET LOST!" IN DC COMICS PRESENTS #3 ON SALE THE FIRST WEEK IN AUGUST!
25

THE ADVENTURES OF

SUPERMAN

WHO IS REALLY THE FASTEST MAN ALIVE? THE MAN OF STEEL OR THE FLASH?

DAN 'N BRETT ALA CARMINE 'N MURPHY

BY JURGENS & THIBERT

YOU KNOW, WALLY, WITH ALL THE MONEY YOU SPEND ON BIG BELLY BURGERS THEY SHOULD PUT YOU IN A COMMERCIAL!
MASON, I'VE DROPPED SO MUCH MONEY AT THESE JOINTS--
--I PROBABLY OWN A FEW OF THEM!

I'LL BET YOU'RE THE ONLY SUPER-HERO ALIVE WHOSE POWER ACTUALLY COSTS MONEY!
TELL ME ABOUT IT.
IF I DIDN'T GET TO CHOW AT THE JUSTICE LEAGUE EMBASSY A COUPLE TIMES A WEEK--
-- MY FOOD BUDGET WOULD RIVAL THE NATIONAL DEBT!
BIG BELLY SPECIAL
HEY, THIS JUST IN, KZAP LISTENERS--

--BELIEVE IT OR NOT, REPORTS INDICATE THERE ARE SOME WILD HAPPENINGS-- PERHAPS EVEN TERRORISTS-- AT MT. RUSHMORE!
MORE ON THAT AFTER THIS FROM THE NEW ROLLING STO--; CLICK;
PROBABLY JUST A BUNCH OF KIDS PAINTING MUSTACHES ON THE FACES.
HOLD THE PHONE HERE, KID! YOU'RE ACTING RATHER CAVALIER ABOUT THIS!

DON'T YOU THINK YOU HAVE A RESPONSIBILITY TO AT LEAST CHECK IT OUT?
CHANCES ARE YOU'RE THE ONLY GUY IN THE MIDWEST WHO CAN HELP IF THERE'S REAL TROUBLE, WALLY!
CHILL OUT, MASON!
JUST THOUGHT I'D FINISH MY GOURMET CUISINE FIRST! AFTER ALL--
--SOUTH DAKOTA--
--IS A FEW HUNDRED MILES AWAY--
--AND I'LL NEED ALL THE CALORIES I CAN GET--
--IF I'M GOING TO SUSTAIN THIS SPEED--
--ONCE I GET THERE!

LESSEE... KEYSTONE CITY TO MT. RUSHMORE... SHOULDN'T TAKE MORE THAN A FEW SECONDS AT THIS SPEED!

COLD OUT HERE. GOOD THING THE AURA THAT PROTECTS ME FROM MY SPEED'S FRICTION WILL HELP AGAINST THE COLD.

-- BUT IT SURE WASN'T *THIS*!
LOOKS LIKE A WHOLE LOTTA POSTCARDS JUST BECAME OBSOLETE!
HEE HEE HEE! QUITE AN IMPROVEMENT, WOULDN'T YOU SAY, RED?
HEY... ALMOST DIDN'T SEE THIS LITTLE FLOATING MAN...
LITTLE FLOATING--?!

PRESIDENT!? SAYYY, THAT'S NOT A BAD IDEA! EH, MAYBE SOMEDAY...
ANYHOO, THE NAME'S MXYZPTLK--*MR.* TO YOU-- PURVEYOR OF GOOD TIMES AND CONSTANT THRILLS!
WHO'RE YOU?
FLASH. PLEASED TO MEET YOU.
I THINK.

FLASH, HUH? SO WHAT DOES A FLASH DO FOR KICKS?
WELL, BESIDES CAVING IN THE SKULLS OF PEOPLE WHO DESECRATE NATIONAL MONUMENTS I RUN FAST.
REAL FAST.
NO *KIDDING*?! FASTER THAN, SAY... SUPERMAN?

WHOA! TERRAIN'S GETTING PRETTY ROUGH AND SLIPPERY. AT LEAST I'M ALMOST THERE.

WILD! I DON'T KNOW WHAT I EXPECTED TO FIND HERE--

SPEED KILLS!

LOOK, PAL-- UNLESS YOU'RE THE PRESIDENT OF OZ, I DOUBT YOUR MUG BELONGS UP THERE!

DAN JURGENS - STORY AND PENCILS
ART THIBERT - FINISHES
ALBERT DE GUZMAN - LETTERS
GLENN WHITMORE - COLORS
JON PETERSON - ASSOCIATE EDITOR
MIKE CARLIN - EDITOR

SUPERMAN CREATED BY
JERRY SIEGEL AND JOE SHUSTER

HOW SHOULD I KNOW? IT'S NOT LIKE WE'VE EVER RUN A RACE OR ANYTHING!
NOW IF YOU DON'T MIND, I WANT SOME ANSWERS!
A RACE?! SAYYY...

PLAY ALONG WITH ME, RED, AND I'LL MAKE YOU A STAR!
LOOK, I DON'T WANNA BE A STAR! I JUST WANT YOUR FACE OFF THAT MOUNTAIN!
GOOD, I KNEW YOU'D SEE IT MY WAY! NEXT STOP--

--METROPOLIS!
HEY, I DON'T WANT TO...
POOF
POOF

METROPOLIS.
AW, C'MON, CHIEF! WHAT DO YOU WANT FROM US?
SIMPLY PUT, AN INFORMATIVE, ENTERTAINING, WELL-ROUNDED NEWS MAGAZINE THAT BEATS THE COMPETITION.

NEWSTIME IS A GOOD, SOLID MAGAZINE BUT IT'S IN A RUT!
COLLIN THORNTON BROUGHT ME OVER TO GIVE NEWSTIME A DYNAMIC NEW LOOK AND THAT'S WHAT WE'RE GOING TO GIVE HIM!
THERE'S SOME PRETTY STIFF COMPETITION OUT THERE, MR. KENT!
AND THAT'S EXACTLY WHY WE HAVE TO BE BETTER!
NATIONAL NEWS
NEWS
TAKE THESE GUYS-- HARD INFORMATION WITH NO FLAIR OR PERSONALITY! IT'S LIKE READING A TELETYPE!
THE MONSTER

WHO NEEDS IT? GET CREATIVE! TAKE CHANCES! AND ONE MORE THING--
--DON'T CALL ME CHIEF!
YES SIR!
YOU GOT IT!
WE'RE WITH YOU, CH--BOSS!

IMPRESSIVE. NOT ONLY ARE YOU AN EXCELLENT WRITER BUT YOU'RE QUITE THE MANAGER AS WELL! LOOKS LIKE I HIRED THE RIGHT MAN!
THANKS, COLLIN, BUT I DON'T THINK WE'LL REALLY KNOW THAT UNTIL WE GET A FEW ISSUES UNDER OUR BELT!

A'EEEE!
SOMEONE SCREAMING IN THE LOBBY!?
WE BETTER NOT HAVE MICE UP HERE AGAIN!
NEWS TIME
NEWS TIME

DO WE CALL SECURITY OR AN EXTERMINATOR?
NEITHER! OUR COMPUTER SYSTEM HAS GONE COMPLETELY BONKERS!
YOU GOTTA SEE IT TO BELIEVE IT!
WHY? OUR COMPUTERS HAVE CERTAINLY CRASHED BEFORE!

I DOUBT THEY EVER CRASHED DUE TO AN INTERDIMENSIONAL OVERLOAD, COLLIN!
I REALIZE THAT YOU JOURNALISTS TRYING TO BEAT A DEADLINE ARE PRETTY FRUSTRATED RIGHT NOW, BUT HANG WITH ME!
MR. MXYZPTLK IS ABOUT TO GIVE YOU THE BIGGEST STORY SINCE EVE MADE THAT DEAL WITH THE SNAKE!

ANNOUNCING THE EVENT OF ALL TIME! A CONTEST OF CHAMPIONS FILLED WITH POWER, SPEED DRAMA, SPEED, EXCITEMENT AND MOST OF ALL--
--TWO REALLY FAST GUYS!
THAT'S THAT MR. WHAT'S-IS-NAME--

WHAT'S THAT IMP BABBLING ABOUT, THIS TIME?
PART OF ME DOESN'T WANT TO KNOW!
OF COURSE I'M TALKING ABOUT A RACE!

A RACE BETWEEN SUPERMAN AND FLASH! THINK ABOUT IT, DREAM ABOUT IT--
--AND CATCH THE START OF IT LIVE IN JUST ONE HOUR AT THE METROPOLIS STADIUM!

COME ONE, COME ALL, ADMISSION IS FREE! HEE HEE HEE!
MUCH AS I'D LIKE TO IGNORE THIS, I CAN'T. IF SUPERMAN DOESN'T MAKE AN APPEARANCE--

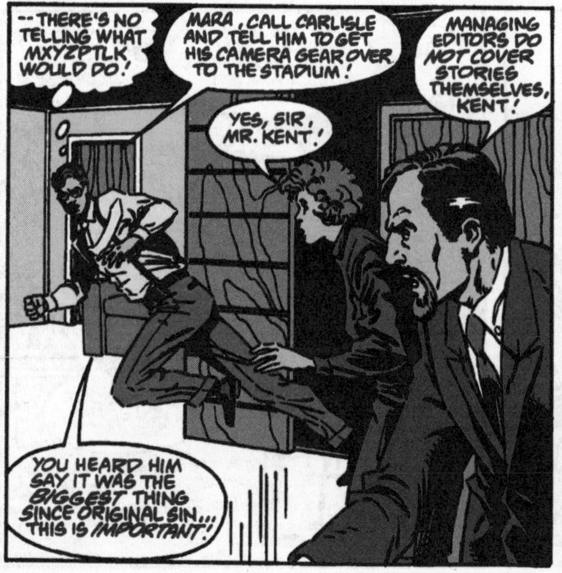
--THERE'S NO TELLING WHAT MXYZPTLK WOULD DO!
MARA, CALL CARLISLE AND TELL HIM TO GET HIS CAMERA GEAR OVER TO THE STADIUM!
YES, SIR, MR. KENT!
MANAGING EDITORS DO NOT COVER STORIES THEMSELVES, KENT!
YOU HEARD HIM SAY IT WAS THE BIGGEST THING SINCE ORIGINAL SIN... THIS IS IMPORTANT!

HATED TO BRUSH THORNTON OFF LIKE THAT, BUT CLARK KENT HAS TO GET OUT OF THE OFFICE--
--IF SUPERMAN'S GOING TO FLY!

LISTEN, I DON'T CARE WHAT YOU SAY! SUPERMAN'S GOT THIS IN THE BAG!
NO WAY, POPS! FLASH BY A MILE!
NO ONE CAN OUTRUN THE BIG "S"!
YOU KIDDIN' ME?! FLASH'LL BLOW HIM AWAY!
WHO CARES WHO WINS? OUGHTA BE A GOOD SHOW!
HEY, MY BOOKIE CARES PLENTY WHO WINS!
VS.
METROPOLIS STADIUM

A RACE?!
BETWEEN SUPERMAN AND ME?!
ARE YOU OUT OF YOUR FREAKING MIND?!

AWW, C'MON, RED! JUST LOOK AT ALL THE PEOPLE HERE WHO WANNA SEE YOU WIN!
FORGET IT, SHORTY!
I'M NOT SOME STUPID PUPPET THAT'S GONNA JUMP JUST CUZ YOU'RE PULLING THE STRINGS!

IF YOU THINK I'M GONNA WASTE MY TIME RACING SUPERMAN--
--YOU'RE NUTS!
GATE F

SIGH

HEY!
HEE HEE. NOW, WHY DON'T YOU PLAY ALONG BEFORE I TURN YOU INTO A TURTLE--
--OR SOMETHING SLOWER?
POOF
HOW ABOUT YOU LEAVE INSTEAD?

GET THROWN OUT OF THE FIFTH DIMENSION FOR SMUGGLING WHOOPEE CUSHIONS AGAIN, MXYZPTLK?
AHH, YOU WOUND ME, SOOPEY! CAN'T YOU SEE THAT I'M PRESENTING YOU WITH THE OPPORTUNITY OF A LIFETIME?
ISN'T THE CHANCE TO PROVE YOUR SUPERIORITY WORTH A HANDSHAKE?
IS THIS CLOWN REALLY A BUDDY OF YOURS?

THIS CLOWN IS JUST THAT-- AND NOTHING MORE.
NOW, IS THAT ANY WAY TO TALK TO THE MAN WHO CAN CLAIM THE FALL OF THE ROMAN EMPIRE ON HIS RESUMÉ?
ARGUE ALL YOU WANT, SUPESTER, BUT YOU KNOW IF I HANG AROUND EARTH LONG I'M LIKELY TO SET OFF AT LEAST FOUR NUCLEAR CONFLICTS.
THAT MEANS YOU SIMPLY HAVE TO GET ME TO RETURN TO MY OWN DIMENSION.
AND IF YOU WANT A SHOT AT THAT--

--YOU GOTTA DANCE TO THE TUNE I PLAY!
SO WHY NOT BE A SPORT AND RACE SPEEDY GONZALEZ OVER THERE? BEAT HIM--
--AND I'M OUTTA YOUR HAIR FOR ANOTHER NINETY DAYS!

BUT IF YOU'D RATHER I STAAYYED...
OKAY, OKAY. BUT WHAT MAKES YOU THINK IT WILL BE MUCH OF A CONTEST?
WORD HAS IT THAT WALLY HERE'S NOT QUITE AS FAST AS THE ORIGINAL FLASH, BARRY ALLEN, WAS--
--AND EVEN THOUGH WE'VE NEVER RACED I KIND OF JUST ASSUMED...
HEY, WAIT A MINUTE!

I MEAN, WHEN YOU GET DOWN TO IT, WHAT WE REALLY HAVE HERE IS A RACE BETWEEN SUPERMAN AND KID FLASH!
ALL RIGHT, THAT'S ENOUGH!

SURE, YOU MIGHT BE ABLE TO MOVE MOUNTAINS AND FLY--
--BUT THAT DOESN'T NECESSARILY MAKE YOU FASTER THAN ME!
I SAY PUT UP OR SHUT UP, SUPERMAN!

LOOK, I DIDN'T MEAN TO INSULT YOU, FLASH! I JUST ASSUMED I WAS NATURALLY FASTER!
LET'S SEE WHAT YOU SAY WHEN I DUST YOU AT THE FINISH LINE!
LADEEEZ AND GENTLEMEN, THE RACE IS ON! HEE HEE HEE!

NOT SO FAST, TINY! WHAT DO I GET OUT OF ALL THIS?
BESIDES THE SATISFACTION OF BEATING OLD SUPES YOU GET A PRIZE SELECTED JUST FOR YOU!
A VERY SPECIAL PRIZE!

NUTS--WHO CARES ABOUT A PRIZE? ALL I KNOW IS THAT IF I BACK OUT OF THIS RACE--
--THE WHOLE WORLD IS GONNA FIGURE ME FOR A WIMPY WEENIE!
JUST HOPE SUPERMAN DOESN'T WHIP ME TOO BAD...
HEE HEE--NOW THAT WE HAVE OUR LINE-UP STRAIGHTENED OUT WE CAN START!
GENTLEMEN--

--START YOUR ENGINES!
WHAT'S WITH THE CARPET?
GROUND RULES, FLASHEROO! THIS IS ACTUALLY THE TRACK YOU TWO WILL RUN THE RACE ON!
NOT ONLY WILL IT MARK THE COURSE FOR YOU, BUT IT'LL HELP ENSURE THAT SUPES DOESN'T FLY!

ONCE AROUND THE WORLD, GENTLEMEN! AND *STEP ON IT!*
ON YOUR MARK--
--GET SET--
B'LAM
--AND GO--
--GO--
--GO!
SUPE
FLASH
SEE YOU AT THE FINISH LINE, SUPERMAN!
GO FLASH!
BETTER HURRY, FLASH! I WON'T WAIT LONG FOR YOU!

CAN'T BELIEVE I'M DOING THIS! BUT IF IT GETS MXYZPTLK OFF MY BACK IT'S WORTH THE PRICE!
THAT IMP IS DANGEROUS! THE LAST TIME HE WAS HERE HE TORE UP HALF OF METROPOLIS!
LOOK AT THE GUY! SO POWERFUL-- SO CONFIDENT--
--IT'S PROBABLY NEVER OCCURRED TO HIM THAT HE JUST MIGHT LOSE!

HURRY IT UP, LOIS!

THE RACE HAS ALREADY *STARTED!*
YOU ARE GOING TO WATCH IT, AREN'T YA?

BE RIGHT THERE, SIS. WHO'S LEADING?
EVEN-STEVEN SO FAR!
OH, I DON'T KNOW, LUCE. I'VE BEEN FEELING SORT OF OUT OF IT ALL WEEK.
I'VE FELT LIKE THIS SINCE CLARK LEFT THE PLANET!
WOW, FOR A SUPERMAN FAN, YOU DON'T SEEM TOO ENTHUSIASTIC!

WOW, LO, I NEVER REALIZED YOU WERE SO HUNG UP ON THE GUY. HE JUST DOESN'T SEEM LIKE YOUR TYPE.
YOU KNOW, HE REALLY IS A PRETTY DECENT GUY! AND EVEN THOUGH I WAS KIND OF HARD ON HIM AT FIRST--
--CLARK WAS ALWAYS THERE FOR ME WHEN I NEEDED HIM!

GUESS I WAS A LITTLE OBSESSED WITH SUPERMAN AND MY CAREER AND JOSE AND EVERYTHING TO REALLY NOTICE HIM.
AND NOW HE'S GONE.

"WE'RE HERE LIVE WITH MR. MASON TROLLBRIDGE, WIDELY REGARDED TO BE A CLOSE ASSOCIATE OF FLASH'S. WHO DO YOU LIKE IN THE BIG RACE, MASON ?"
"WELL, I FIGURE FLASH'S ODDS ARE PRETTY GOOD SO LONG AS WE CAN GET PEOPLE TO HELP US OUT BY GIVING FLASH FOOD ALONG THE COURSE. KIND OF LIKE MARATHON RUNNERS GET, YOU KNOW."

"THANKS, MASON. WE'RE SWITCHING TO A REMOTE SECTION OF NORTH DAKOTA WHERE HUNDREDS OF PEOPLE ARE DOING JUST AS MR. TROLLBRIDGE SUGGESTS. REPORTS FROM SOUTH DAKOTA SAY THE RUNNERS ARE APPROACHING--"

"--YES... HERE THEY COME AND... WOOOO... THERE THEY GO!"
THANKS FOR THE OFFER, BUT I DON'T NEED ANY FOOD!
GREAT! JUST WHAT THE DOCTOR ORDERED!

WHY DON'T YOU HAVE TO EAT, SUPERMAN ? YOU'RE EXPENDING ENERGY SAME AS ME!
MY KRYPTONIAN CELLS ABSORB AND BURN THE ENERGY OF THE SUN!
GUESS I JUST "EAT" IN A MORE DIRECT FASHION!

YA HOO-- NECK AND NECK, EH ?
REMEMBER, I'LL BE WATCHING ALL THE WAY! AND IF ANYBODY CHEATS--
--WHAMMO!
IS THAT TWERP FOR REAL ?
UNFORTUNATELY...

¡SIGH¡--THIS IS ALREADY GETTING BORING! MAYBE I SHOULD LIVEN THINGS UP!

SO, MXYZPTLK IS REALLY FROM ANOTHER DIMENSION?
YEAH. HE SHOWS UP EVERY NOW AND THEN LOOKING FOR FUN... BY WAY OF CREATING HAVOC! AND SINCE HIS POWERS DEFY OUR DIMENSIONAL LAWS--
--MY OWN POWERS ARE PRETTY MUCH USELESS AGAINST HIM.

NO WONDER YOU HAVE TO MAKE BARGAINS TO GET RID OF--

YEEOWW!
THIS FREAKY COURSE HAS COME ALIVE--
--LIKE IT'S TRYING TO SHAKE US OFF!
IT'S MXYZPTLK'S WAY OF MAKING THINGS MORE INTERESTING!

WHY ELSE WOULD THE COURSE RUN ALONG THE FLOOR OF THE BERING STRAIT?
I CAN'T RUN UNDERWATER! WHAT'LL I DO?

ONE CHANCE--I'M GONNA TRY RUNNING ON THE SURFACE... LIKE A ROCK SKIPPING THE WAVES!

¡UHHH¡--LOSING BALANCE--LOOK OUT!

NEVER REALLY TRIED RUNNING THIS FAR OR TESTING MY ENDURANCE BEFORE--
--BUT I'M SURE I CAN BEAT FLASH! AFTER ALL, HE'S ONLY A HUMAN!

OOF!--THE TECHNIQUE MAY NOT LOOK PRETTY BUT IT GOT THE JOB DONE!
HEY, SHOULDN'T YOU BE DISQUALIFIED FOR LEAVING THE COURSE?

WRONGO, SUPES! FLASHEROO'S TOOTSIES NEVER *LEFT GOOD OL'* EARTH--HE WAS IN CONTACT WITH *TERRA INFIRMA* THE WHOLE TIME!
THEREFORE, AS THE COMPLETELY IMPARTIAL REFEREE OF THIS EVENT, I'M NOT GONNA PENALIZE HIM JUST 'CAUSE HE CAN'T MAKE LIKE A FISH WHEN YOU CAN!
AND ACCORDING TO THE RULES, WHICH I'M MAKING UP AS YOU GO ALONG, FROM NOW ON YOU'RE ON *SEPARATE TRACKS*!
JEEZ, THANKS, MIXXY. YOU'RE A REAL PEACH!

BARRY ALWAYS SPOKE SO HIGHLY OF SUPERMAN--MADE HIM OUT TO BE SO POWERFUL THAT I WAS ALMOST INTIMIDATED BY HIM!
BUT WE'RE STILL EVEN UP! MAYBE I REALLY *CAN* WIN THIS THING!
HEE HEE, I MUST ADMIT THAT I DO LOVE DRIVING SUPES NUTSO!
WHOA-HO-HO, WHAT'S THAT?! DO MY PEEPERS DECEIVE ME--
--OR DO I SEE SOMEONE ELSE I KNOW?

OUR SATELLITE SENSORS TRACKED THE METEOR TO THIS APPROXIMATE LOCATION, SIR!
EXCELLENT. IF THERE IS ANY *KRYPTONITE* EMBEDDED IN THE METEOR WE'LL EXTRACT IT AND RETREAT.
EVEN SOMEONE OF MY *STATURE* WOULD HAVE TROUBLE EXPLAINING MY PRESENCE TO SOVIET AUTHORITIES!
OLD FRIEND, OLD BUDDY, OLD PAL, IS IT REALLY *YOU*?

YES, YES IT IS! LEX LUTHOR!
ALL YOU HAD TO DO WAS ASK AND I WOULD GLADLY HAVE GIVEN YOU A RINGSIDE SEAT!
GET AWAY FROM ME, YOU IGNOMINIOUS LITTLE TOAD!
I DON'T KNOW WHAT YOU'RE BABBLING ABOUT AND I DON'T CARE! AND IF YOU PLAN TO HARASS ME AS YOU DID BEFORE I'LL KILL YOU!

GADZOOKS! HOW CAN THIS BE?
HOW CAN THE GREAT LEX LUTHOR NOT KNOW OF THE GREAT RACE!?
MY CONCERNS ARE MY OWN, MXYZPTLK. LEAVE US!
NO SIGNS OF ANY KRYPTONITE IN THE AREA, SIR. WE MIGHT AS WELL LEAVE.

KRYPTONITE, HMM? Y'KNOW, LEX, I'D LIKE TO MAKE UP FOR THE TROUBLES I CAUSED YOU IN THE PAST!
I WAS GONNA GIVE THIS SPECIAL PRIZE TO FLASH--

--BUT I THINK MAYBE YOU COULD USE IT MORE.
SNAP

WHATCHA THINK? PEACE? PEACE OF KRYP'TONITE?

GOOD THING WE HAVE THESE RADIATION SUITS ON, BOSS. IT'S NOT GREEN K, BUT THAT ROCK IS PRETTY RICH!
WRONG COLOR? WELL, IT WAS A GOOD GUESS... NO?
MXYZPTLK, YOU ARE A FOOL! GET THAT WORTHLESS CHUNK OF POISON OUT OF HERE!

WORTHLESS, HUH?
OH, FUDGE.

LET'S MOVE ON TO THE NEXT SITE, REYNOLDS!
ONLY SUPERMAN RAISES MY IRE MORE THAN THAT IMP!
LOVE TO JOIN YOU, LEXXY, BUT I'VE GOT A RACE TO GET BACK TO--

"--AND THOSE TWO CHUCKLEHEADS ARE PROBABLY IN THE SOVIET UNION'S URAL MOUNTAIN RANGE, BY NOW."
WHEW-- I'M ACTUALLY STARTING TO FEEL A BIT WINDED!
EVEN THOUGH I HAVE SUPER-HUMAN POWERS I'M NOT TRAINED AS A RUNNER AND THIS IS MORE PHYSICAL WORK THAN FLYING TO THE MOON!
AT LEAST I'VE MOVED OUT FRONT! THE LACK OF AIR AT THIS ALTITUDE IS REALLY HARD ON FLASH!
MAN, LOOK AT BIG-BLUE GO! I GOTTA KEEP BREATHING UP HERE WHILE HE'S STILL GOT A LUNG FULL OF THE GOOD STUFF!
SHOULD'VE KNOWN THAT I WAS OUTCLASSED FROM THE START-- THAT I HAD NO CHANCE!
AND NOW THE WHOLE WORLD IS GONNA SEE ME LOSE--
--UNLESS I CAN REALLY POUR IT ON... GET A SECOND WIND AND PROVE I DESERVE TO WEAR BARRY'S UNIFORM!
AMAZING! FLASH IS STARTING TO CLOSE THE GAP DESPITE THE LACK OF OXYGEN!
HAVE TO STAY IN FRONT--NOT JUST TO GET RID OF MXYZPTLK--
--BUT BECAUSE I'D REALLY HATE TO LOSE!
SKRUNNNK
YEOWW! NOW WHAT?

HI, GUYS! I'M BAAAACK!
HEY, PUT ME DOWN! I'M RUNNING YOUR BLASTED RACE-- WHAT MORE DO YOU WANT?
HE'S JUST TRYING TO REMIND US WHO'S IN CHARGE OF THIS SHOW!
HEE HEE HEE! NOW, THIS IS ENTERTAINMENT!

SHALL WE CONTINUE?
IF YOU THINK YOU CAN STILL KEEP UP-- LET'S DO IT!

PARIS, FRANCE.
STATUS REPORT, METAMORPHO!
SO FAR, SO GOOD, CAP! TWINKLE TOES IS REALLY HANGIN' IN THERE!
GO, FLASH, GO! FOR HONOR-- FOR GLORY--

--FOR THE SAKE OF JUSTICE LEAGUE EUROPE--BEAT SUPERMAN!
PERSONALLY, I HOPE SUPERMAN RUNS HIM RIGHT OUT OF THOSE WIMPY, WINGED BOOTS.

NEW YORK, NEW YORK.
THE RACE PROCEEDS AS EXPECTED, MR. MIRACLE. THE CONTESTANTS ARE DEPARTING THE SOVIET UNION EVEN AS WE SPEAK.
WAY TO KICK, FLASH! RUN LIKE YOU'VE NEVER RUN BEFORE!
BOOSTER, ARE YOU CRAZY? WE'RE SUPPOSED TO BE CHEERING SUPERMAN HERE!

WE DON'T WANT SOME REPRESENTATIVE FROM THAT GANG OF SECOND-RATE IMITATORS TO WIN!
GIMME A BREAK, BEETLE! I GOT A THOUSAND BUCKS ON FLASH AT FOUR TO ONE ODDS!

EGYPT.
<DO THEY APPROACH?>
<YES, PRAISE ALLAH! I BELIEVE I SEE THEM!>
<FAH! IT IS MORE LIKELY A SANDSTORM!>

< NO, INFIDEL! IT TRULY IS THE SPECIAL ONES! >
THANKS A LOT, FRIEND! I'M TIRED ENOUGH-- WITHOUT THIS FOOD I'D NEVER FINISH THE RACE!
EVERY TIME I THINK I HAVE YOU BEAT YOU MANAGE TO BOUNCE BACK!

HEY, IF I COULDN'T DO THAT THEY WOULDN'T CALL ME FLASH!
YOU MIGHT WEAR THE CLOTHES BUT YOU'RE NOT THE HUMBLE MAN BARRY WAS!

WHY CAN'T ANY OF YOU OLD GUYS GO FIVE MINUTES WITHOUT MENTIONING HIM?
HE WAS A GOOD MAN, WALLY. YOU'VE GOT A LOT TO LIVE UP--

BRKAMM
...UHN!... THAT TUNNEL--
--IT WAS JUST AN ILLUSION! REALLY SOLID ROCK--!

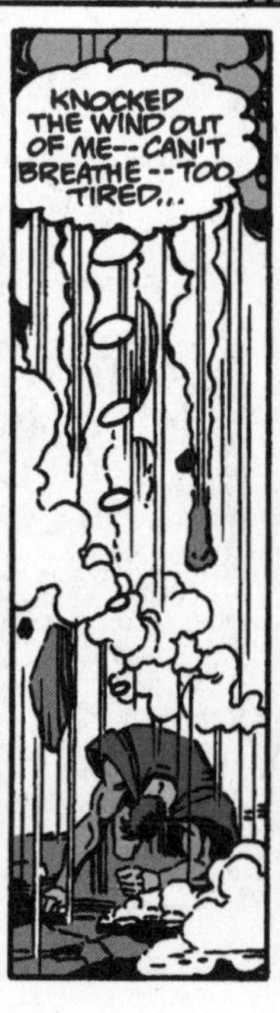
KNOCKED THE WIND OUT OF ME--CAN'T BREATHE--TOO TIRED...

LOOKS LIKE THE WHOLE CAVE COLLAPSED AND BURIED SUPERMAN!
IF IT TAKES HALF AS LONG AS IT LOOKS LIKE IT WILL FOR HIM TO DIG OUT I'VE GOT THIS SUCKER LOCKED UP!

JEEZ, WHAT IF SOMETHING'S REALLY WRONG, THOUGH, AND HE CAN'T DIG OUT?
STRONG AS HE IS, HE HIT THAT ROCK HARD AND FAST! EVEN IF HE IS INVULNERABLE-- HE'S BEEN RUNNING FOR A WHILE... PROBABLY PRETTY BEAT TO START WITH.
BESIDES, IF MXYZPTLK RIGGED THAT THING WITH HIS PSEUDO-MAGIC, WHO KNOWS HOW IT AFFECTED SUPERMAN?
NO CHOICE.

GOTTA GET MOVIN'--
--AND USE MY SPEED--
--ALONG WITH A LITTLE ELBOW GREASE--
--TO DIG DOWN TO THE BOTTOM--
--AND GET HIM OUT OF THERE BEFORE THE SAND FLEAS START CRAWLING UP HIS CAPE!

WELCOME BACK TO THE LAND OF THE LIVING!
YEAH--LOOKS LIKE MXYZPTLK IS OUT TO RIG THE RACE!
SPEAKING OF WHICH, I'M SURPRISED YOU'RE STILL AROUND!

HEY, EVERY NOW AND THEN I CAN'T HELP MYSELF. I DO A GOOD DEED.
RIGHT. LOOK, YOU PROBABLY DON'T WANT TO HEAR THIS, BUT I THINK BARRY WOULD BE PRETTY HAPPY TO SEE YOU IN HIS GEAR.

MAYBE IT'S TIME YOU ACCEPT THAT.
UM... YEAH, WELL... WHAT SAY WE GET MOVING--
--AND GET BACK TO THE RACE? I STILL DO INTEND TO WIN.
SO DO I.

WHEW--CAN'T BELIEVE THIS PACE! NEVER RUN THIS FAST--THIS FAR BEFORE--

--AND WE STILL GOTTA GO THROUGH SPAIN AND ACROSS THE ATLANTIC!
EXHAUSTED--LEGS ARE LIKE SPAGHETTI! FLASH IS FASTER--STRONGER THAN I THOUGHT!

AND I FEEL LIKE--I MIGHT NOT EVEN BE ABLE TO FINISH!

HOW ABOUT THAT, JAY? LOOKS LIKE OUR YOUNG FELLOW IS DOING US PROUD!

C'MON, WALLY! SHOW LI'L OL' CONNIE HOW MUCH YOU LOVE HER!

WOW, LOIS! THOSE GUYS ARE STILL IN A DEAD HEAT!
AND I THOUGHT FOR SURE THAT SUPERMAN WAS A CINCH TO WIN!

ANY SIGN OF THEM YET, CHIEF?
SHOULDN'T BE LONG, JIMMY!
I HOPE THEY HURRY--I'M FREEZING OUT HERE!

BOY, ISN'T THAT SUMTHIN? ALL THE WAY AROUND THE WORLD...
RUN, CLARK, RUN!

WONDER HOW LOIS WILL FEEL ABOUT HIM IF FLASH KICKS HIS BUTT?

GOODNESS GRACIOUS! THEY'RE RUNNING AT SEVERAL TIMES THE SPEED OF SOUND!

WHERE THE DEVIL IS KENT? THE BIGGEST STORY OF THE YEAR--AND MY MANAGING EDITOR DISAPPEARS!

YIPPEE KIII--YAYYY, GENTLEMEN! YOU ARE NOW ENTERING THE HOME STRETCH!
WHO WILL WIN?
WHO WILL LOSE?
STAY TUNED--FILM AT ELEVEN! HEE HEE!
MXYZPTLK--

--SHUT THE HECK UP!
SPALOOSH

STILL HALF THE ATLANTIC TO GO--AND I CAN'T SHAKE HIM!
NEVER THOUGHT I COULD EVEN RUN THIS ;PANT;--FAST! AND I STILL CAN'T PASS HIM!

LUNGS BURNING--LEGS ACHING--SO TIRED--;PANT;--I JUST WANT TO DROP!
EXPECTED TO BE ON CRUISE CONTROL BY NOW--BUT I MUST GO FASTER!

CAN'T BELIEVE--PANT--I'M STILL RUNNING NECK AND NECK WITH SUPERMAN!
BUT I FEEL LIKE I'VE GOT NUTHIN' LEFT--AND HE'S SPEEDING UP!

BLAST IT, SUPERMAN! WHY DON'T YOU DROP?!
PACK IT IN, FLASH! GIVE IT UP!
CAN'T YOU SEE I HAVE TO GET RID OF MXYZPTLK?

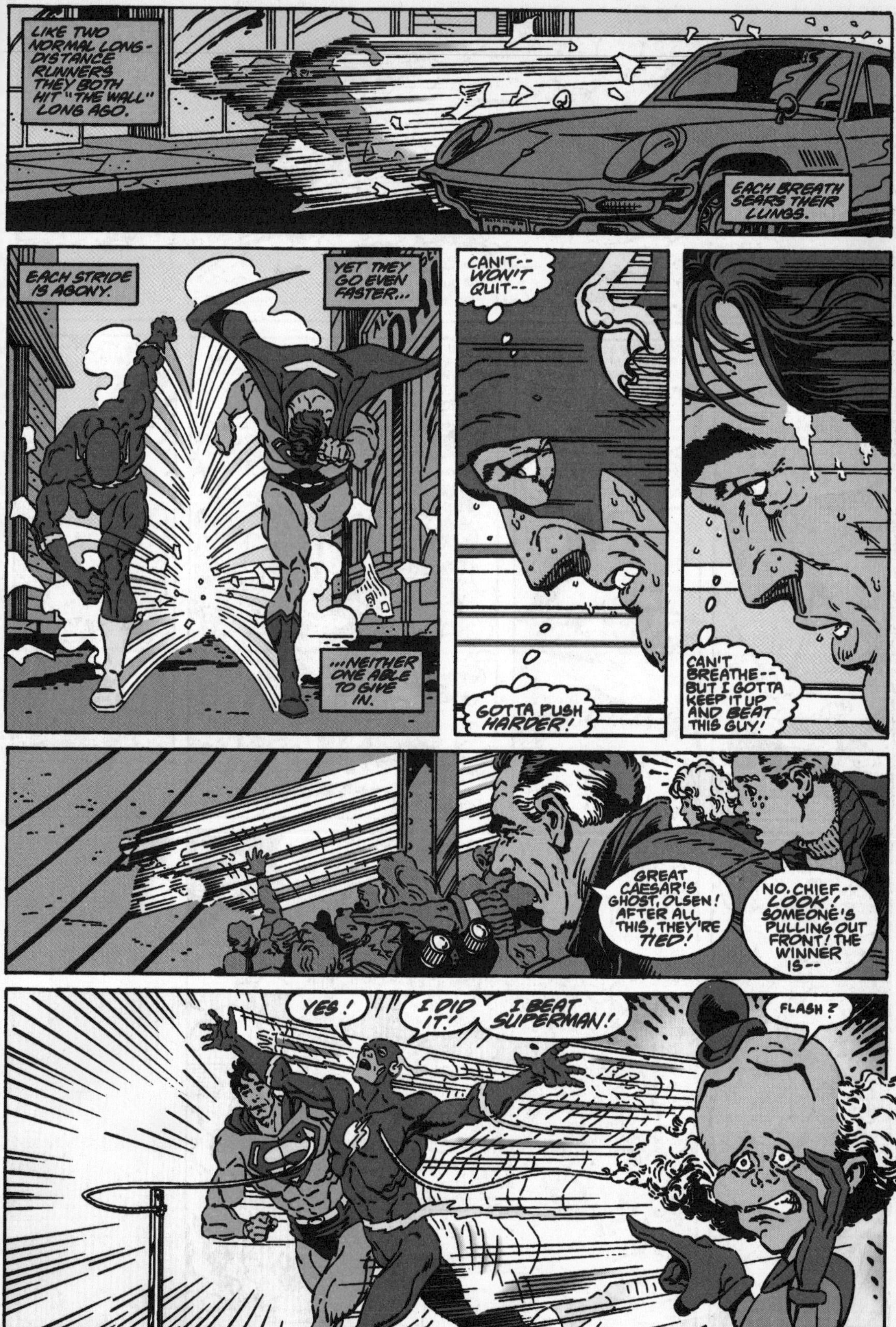

LIKE TWO NORMAL LONG-DISTANCE RUNNERS THEY BOTH HIT "THE WALL" LONG AGO.

EACH BREATH SEARS THEIR LUNGS.

EACH STRIDE IS AGONY.

YET THEY GO EVEN FASTER...

...NEITHER ONE ABLE TO GIVE IN.

CAN'T-- WON'T QUIT--

GOTTA PUSH *HARDER!*

CAN'T BREATHE-- BUT I GOTTA KEEP IT UP AND *BEAT* THIS GUY!

GREAT CAESAR'S GHOST, OLSEN! AFTER ALL THIS, THEY'RE *TIED!*

NO, CHIEF-- *LOOK!* SOMEONE'S PULLING OUT FRONT! THE WINNER IS--

I DON'T GET IT! I LOST!
CONSARN IT! #@☆○*○ FLASH WON!
I DON'T KNOW HOW THE #@☆○○!☆ HE DID IT, BUT HE WON!
'N' NOW I GOTTA GO HOME! THANKS FER NUTHIN', LUTHOR!

LAST TIME I WAS HERE LUTHOR LIED TO ME-- HE SHOWED ME HOW TO SET UP A FALSE DEAL!
AND SINCE I KNEW YOU WERE A SHOE-IN TO WIN THE RACE, I WAS ONLY PLANNIN' TO LEAVE IF FLASH WON!
I'M A BAAAD LIAR!

SOMEHOW YOU SAW THROUGH MY TRICK AND THREW THE RACE!
I MUST'VE MISSED SOME SUBTLETY IN LUTHOR'S TECHNIQUE!
SO EVEN THOUGH YOU LOST THE STUPID RACE, SUPERDOPE--

--YOU WIN BECAUSE I HAVE TO ABIDE BY MY OWN RULES AND GO!
I SHOULD HAVE KNOWN IT WOULDN'T BE EASY TO LIE TO MYSELF!
BUT I'M GOING TO PRACTICE--AND THEN I'LL BE BACK!
POOF
THANK GOD!

DAMN IT, SUPERMAN--
--YOU KNEW! YOU FOLDED AND LET ME WIN!

ARE YOU KIDDING ME? :HUFF: I HAD NO IDEA WHAT HE WAS UP TO! :PUFF: I GAVE THAT RACE EVERYTHING I HAD ...AND MORE!
YOU WON IT FAIR AND SQUARE, PAL!

I'D SAY YOU'RE PROBABLY THE FASTEST MAN ALIVE!
WELL, HOW ABOUT THAT!
THERE'S ONLY ONE PROBLEM!
WHAT'S THAT?
THAT LITTLE TWERP LEFT WITHOUT GIVING ME MY PRIZE!
END

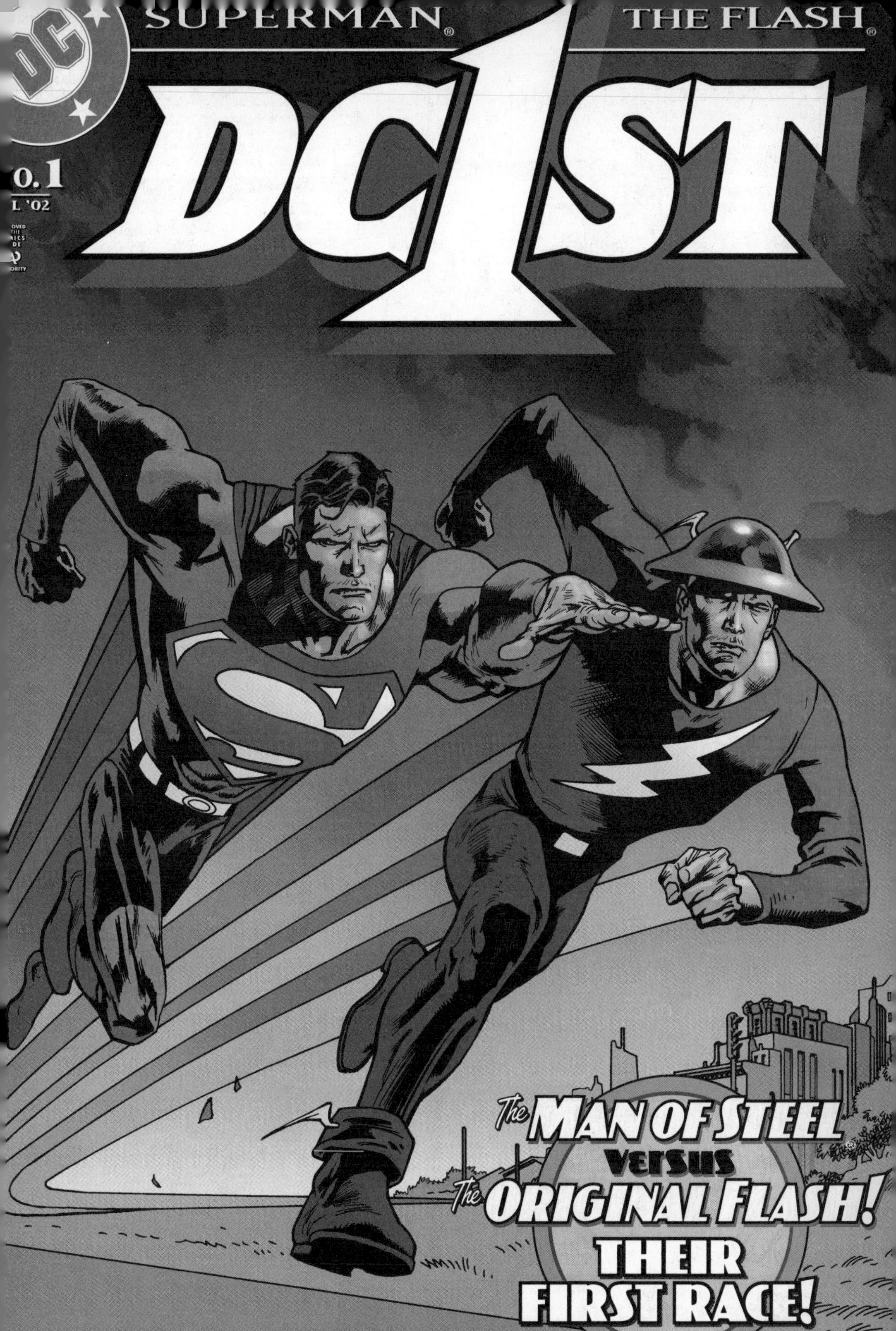

SUPERMAN
THE FLASH
DC
DC 1ST
The MAN OF STEEL
versus
The ORIGINAL FLASH!
THEIR
FIRST RACE!
GEOFF JOHNS
RICK BURCHETT
PRENTIS ROLLINS
K. Nowlan

KEYSTONE CITY.
IRON HEIGHTS PENITENTIARY.
KNOWN TO MANY AS "THE ROGUE FACTORY."
*These events take place before "CROSSFIRE" Between IMPULSE #84 and THE FLASH #184 to be exact!
--REMEMBER THE DAY BEFORE?
NO.
DO YOU KNOW WHY YOU WENT TO VISIT YOUR PARENTS?
...
THE POLICE RECOVERED SOME INFORMATION OFF YOUR COMPUTER. AN E-MAIL FROM YOUR FATHER, ASKING FOR HELP. SAYING HE COULDN'T COVER FOR YOU ANYMORE.
SO?
WHAT DID HE MEAN?
LOOK, I'M ONLY HERE TO HELP YOU, MR. RATHAWAY. THE FLASH ASKED ME TO LOOK INTO YOUR CASE, SO I AM.
HE SAYS YOU'VE BEEN FRAMED FOR THE MURDER OF YOUR PARENTS--
--BUT YOU HAVE TO START TALK--
FWEET
FWEET FWEET
THAT'S PRETTY.
ONE THING I DO REMEMBER.
MUSIC. PLAYING MUSIC.
DO YOU LIKE MUSIC, OFFICER ZOLOMON?
NOT ESPECIALLY.
THEN I DON'T THINK WE'RE GOING TO GET ALONG.

KRAK
NNG.
FFWWMPP!
THANK YOU, OFFICER.
FWWAK
WHAT? WHAT ARE YOU TALKING A--
ARRR.
SNPP

OKAY. INTERROGATION'S OVER, HUNTER.

THE *PIED PIPER'S* GOIN' *BACK* INTA HIS CELL... AND HE'S GONNA GET A *VISIT* FROM THE WARDEN LATER TODAY. SOON AS HE GETS BACK FROM HIS *LUNCH* WITH THE GOVERNOR.

BET YOU LOOK *FORWARD* TO THAT, DON'TCHA, PIPER?

TOLD YOU, YA SHOULDN'T HAVE MET WITH PIPER UNACCOMPANIED. HE'S *NUTS*.

I'M NOT SO *SURE*.

YOU *STILL* WANT TO *PROFILE* THE *OTHER* GUY? WE COULD SCHEDULE IT TOMORROW OR--

NO. I NEED TO CHECK OUT *AMNESIA* VICTIM NUMBER *TWO*.
SUPPOSEDLY, HIS MIND WAS WIPED *CLEAN* AND HIS *POWERS* HAVE VANISHED. I WANT TO MAKE SURE HE'S NOT PLAYING *POSSUM*.
TAKE ME TO THE *PIPE-LINE*.

DAMN RATS!
FWWP!!
SO... THIS OTHER WEIRDO'S STORY TRUE?
EXCUSE ME?
IS IT TRUE? THAT, YOU KNOW...
THAT HE'S A CRIMINAL FROM THE SIXTY-FOURTH CENTURY?
HE CLAIMS TO BE. AND THE FLASH HAS SAID HE'S EVEN BEEN THERE.
I LOVE SCIENCE FICTION AND ALL, BUT TIME TRAVEL?
LOOK, WE CAN'T PROVE ANYTHING.
THAT "FUTURE" THE FLASH VISITED MAY HAVE BEEN AN ILLUSION OF SOME SORT.
THIS MAN COULD JUST BE ANOTHER PARANOID HOMICIDAL MANIAC--
--WHO HAPPENS TO KNOW A THING OR TWO ABOUT TECHNOLOGICAL MAGIC.
DO YOU REALLY THINK SO? YOU THINK HE'S JUST A DELUSIONAL FREAK?
THAT THE SCHIZO MADE ALL THAT FUTURE STUFF UP?
ABRA KADABRA
I...

I'M NOT SURE EVEN HE KNOWS ANYMORE.
SPEEDING BULLETS
GEOFF JOHNS, writer
RICK BURCHETT, penciller
PRENTIS ROLLINS, inker
JOHN COSTANZA, letterer
JAMES SINCLAIR, colorist
DIGITAL CHAMELEON, separator
JOEY CAVALIERI, editor

WHO AM I?
THAT'S WHAT I'M HERE TO FIND OUT, MY NAME IS HUNTER ZOLOMON. I WORK FOR THE KEYSTONE POLICE DEPARTMENT.
I...
DO I KNOW YOU?
STEP BACK, PAL.
WHY ISN'T HE SECURED?
WE STRIPPED HIM OF EVERY TECHNO-GADGET WE COULD FIND, HAD DOZENS OF COMPUTER CIRCUITS IMPLANTED UNDERNEATH HIS SKIN.
HELL, DON'T WORRY. NOT EVEN HOUDINI HIMSELF COULD SNEAK OUTTA THIS CELL.
HOUDINI... OF COURSE.
IT'S ALWAYS ABOUT HOUDINI.
Door:
ABRA KADABRA.
WHO AM I?

CHOOM
SHRRRP!
THE TRICKS I'VE PERFORMED AROUND THE WORLD! YET IT'S HOUDINI THAT PEOPLE REMEMBER.
KELLAR. BLACKSTONE. CARTER THE @#&%! "GREAT." THE IDIOTS.
I REMEMBER NOW. I AM THE GREATEST MAGICIAN IN THE WORLD.
Skin.
ABRA KADABRA.
THE MOST AMAZING SHOW-MAN OF ALL PAST AND FUTURE.
LADIES AND GENTLEMEN, I PRESENT TO YOU--
SFFT! SFFT!

..ABRA KADABRA!
REMOVING MY CIRCUIT-GRAFTS DOES NOT SEPARATE ME FROM MY POWER NOR CUT OFF ACCESS TO MY PROPS, OFFICER.
NOW WHERE IS THAT SUPER-SPACE TIME-FOLD...
NN. HOW...
Wand.
ABRA KADABRA.
SWOOOM!
AH, YES. JUST WHERE I LEFT IT.
YOU'D BE AMAZED AT WHAT SIXTY-FOURTH CENTURY SCIENCE IS CAPABLE OF.
IT'S LIKE MAGIC.

WE'VE GOT A BREAK-OUT! I NEED ALL AVAILABLE UNITS DOWN TO THE PIPELINE! I REPEAT--
THIS FOR EXAMPLE.
NOTHING UP MY SLEEVE...
SSSHUNNNK!
ZINNG
MY DEAR FRIEND. YOU'LL LOVE THIS TRICK. IT'S TRULY A CLASSIC.
NO. DON'T--
ABRA KADABRA.
SSSHRRKHKK!
WELL DONE, KADABRA. BRILLIANT!
KLAP KLAP!
O'NEIL, THOMAS
THE TOP

WHY, THANK YOU, TOP. YOUR APPLAUSE IS MOST APPRECIATED.
AND NOW, ANOTHER CLASSIC.
FWOOM!

♪ Pop goes the weas-el! ♫
COOL!
BWOINNNG!
KRAKOWW!
KRKK
ABRA KADABRA!

KLAP KLAP KLAP KLAP KLAP

THANK YOU. THANK YOU *ALL* SO VERY VERY MUCH.

DID YOU ENJOY THE *SHOW*?

I'M NOT AFRAID OF YOU.

HH... I SEE IT NOW. I'M *NOT* GOING TO *PERFORM* A *TRICK* ON YOU, *FRIEND*. THERE'S SOMETHING *ELSE*...
YOUR *FUTURE* ...

I'LL BE ROOTING FOR YOU.
FWOOSH!

HONNK!
METRO
MEEP MEEP!
KAFFF--!
FFZZZSH
YOU'RE LAGGING A LITTLE, JAY. WHAT'S WRONG?
GETTING TIRED?
I'M NOT TIRED.
FZZSH
FZZZZZZSH!
METROPOLIS
NEXT LEFT

FZZZSSSH!
HEY, YOU KNOW I'M JUST KIDDING, RIGHT?
DON'T WORRY ABOUT ME, WALLY. IT'S JUST...
JOAN.
I LOVE HER. AND TO SEE MY WIFE FACE SOMETHING I CAN'T FIGHT DIRECTLY...
THAT CANCER.
IT'S AFFECTING ME... MORE THAN I REALIZED, I GUESS.
YOU KNOW... I SHOULD LOOK LIKE I'M IN MY EIGHTIES.
BUT BECAUSE OF THIS... STRANGE ENERGY WE TAP INTO, THE SPEED FORCE THAT LETS US OUTRUN LIGHTNING... I LOOK... WHAT?
FIFTY?
IF THAT. MORE LIKE FORTY-FIVE.
IT'S DAMN TOUGH. TO OUTLIVE YOUR FRIENDS AND FAMILY. MOST OF THE ORIGINAL MEMBERS OF THE JUSTICE SOCIETY OF AMERICA ARE GONE.
I'VE BEEN ABLE TO COPE WITH IT SO FAR. EVEN WHEN OUR ADOPTED BABY DIED.
BUT ONLY BECAUSE I HAD JOAN TO HELP ME THROUGH IT ALL.
LOSING MY WIFE... I DON'T KNOW IF I CAN SURVIVE THIS.
DON'T KNOW IF I WANT TO.

LAURA'S USED BOOKS

JUST BE GLAD THE SPEED FORCE HASN'T AFFECTED YOUR AGING AS IT HAS MINE.

THIS IS THE STORE. ONLY PLACE I COULD FIND IT.

SKEEEEEEE

WHOA! THAT'S THE FLASH! BOTH OF THEM!

HEY, THERE.

YOU SAID YOU'RE HAPPY WITH THE DOCTOR THAT JOAN'S SEEING IN DENVER.

SO FAR. VERY. BUT THIS TYPE OF LEUKEMIA IS RARE ...AND ALMOST IMPOSSIBLE TO TREAT.

JOAN'S PUT ON SUCH A BRAVE FACE. AND IMPULSE... BART'S PRESENCE SHOULD DO HER SOME GOOD.

SHE DOES LOVE CHILDREN.
YOU'RE THE FLASH. JAY GARRICK. THE FIRST ONE. YOU KNOW... FROM "THE GOLDEN AGE" AND ALL...
CAN I... CAN I HELP YOU?
AND WALLY WEST! THE CURRENT FLASH.

WOW. BOTH OF YOU. HERE IN MY STORE.
HI. I CALLED EARLIER ABOUT A BOOK. YOU HELD IT UNDER "JAY."

OH, YES! YOU'RE JAY. OF COURSE... IT'S MY ONLY COPY. HARD BOOK TO FIND. JOHNNY MOUSE AND THE WISHING STICK.
NEXT TO RAGGEDY ANN AND ANDY, GRUELLE'S BEST IN MY OPINION.

IT WAS MY WIFE'S FAVORITE WHEN SHE WAS A CHILD. THIS WILL MEAN A LOT TO HER.
HOW MUCH DO I OWE YOU?

YOU? OH, DON'T WORRY ABOUT--
FWTCH! FWTCH! FWTCH!
WHA--?

SKREE!
SKREEE!
SKREEE!
AAH!
GET DOWN, MISS.
WHAT'S HAPPENING?!
SSHEEEEEK
WALLS ARE TURNING INTO PLAYING CARDS.
A HOUSE OF CARDS...
IT'S COLLAPSING!
NOT ON US.
FWOOOSH
GOOD EVENING.
FWOOOSH

ABRA-KADABRA
WE HAVE AN AMAZING NIGHT PLANNED. SIMPLY AMAZING.
JOIN THE CROWD, WALLY.
KLAP KLAP KLAP KLAP KLAP
DON'T BE SHY.
TERRIFIC. I WAS HOPING THIS GUY WAS LOBOTOMIZED PERMANENTLY. LAST TIME I SAW HIM, PLASTIC MAN WAS YANKING SOME MIND-CONTROLLING ALIEN OUT HIS NOSE.
WHY'S EVERYONE CLAPPING?
THEY DON'T HAVE A CHOICE. DO THEY, ABRA KADA-BRA?
YOU KNOW, I'LL NEVER GET TIRED OF HEARING YOU SPEAK MY NAME, FLASH.
SENDS CHILLS DOWN MY SPINE.

HOW... ADORABLE. DON'T YOU *ALL* THINK?

FWOOOSHHH

KLAP KLAP KLAP

WHAT DO YOU WANT, KADABRA?

KLAP

KLAP

Rabbits.

ABRA-KADABRA.

RARRAAAA

RRAHH

I'LL DO *ANYTHING* TO BE *REMEMBERED*.

RAAARR
AH. LADIES AND GENTLEMEN, BOYS AND GIRLS. A ROUND OF APPLAUSE FOR THE MAN OF STEEL-- SUPERMAN!
I'VE GOT THEM, FLASH.
KLP KLP KLP KLP
VWOOOSHH
GET OFF... MY STAGE!
ZZWPP
EARS PICKED UP THE RUCKUS. IT'S GOOD TO SEE YOU AND JAY IN METROPOLIS, FLASH. BUT, ABRA KADABRA?
YOUR PERFORMANCE IS OVER.
SILLY MAN. THIS IS JUST THE PRE-SHOW!
ARRRR!
VZZZXXH

WALLY!
NNR
KRRAKK
WALLY ARE YOU--
FLASH!
WHAT... KAFF
WHAT'S WRONG WITH ME?
WHAT DID YOU--
IN THIS AGE OF HEROES, STAGE MAGIC IS A LOST ART. I'M HERE TO RETURN IT TO ITS FORMER GLORY.
KRSHH!
YOUR FRIEND AND MINE, THE FLASH, WILL BE DEAD OF OLD AGE IN LESS THAN FIVE MINUTES.
I'VE CURSED HIM. A MAGIC SPELL I PICKED UP FROM A GYPSY IN--
WILL YOU STOP, SUPERMAN. IT'S REALLY QUITE ANNOYING.
FZZZZ

Run.

ABRA KADABRA.

GGN.

WALLY!

ABRA KADABRA'S
GREAT RACE
KLPP! KLPP!
KLPP! KLPP!
VOOOMMP
STOP
NOW IF YOU WOULD KINDLY LEND ME YOUR EARS, GENTLEMEN.
I'VE PUT A SPELL ON MY AUDIENCE AS I HAVE THE FLASH. THE ONLY WAY TO REVERSE THEIR AGING, AND RETURN THEM TO NORMAL, IS TO OUTRUN THE FASTEST MAN ALIVE.
SO... GET IN POSITION, ACTORS!
ABRA KADABRA.
ARR. C-CAN'T MOVE.
VOOOM!
NOW HERE'S THE TRICK. THE FIRST OF YOU TO TOUCH FLASH WILL SAVE EVERYONE.
BUT THE "WINNER" WILL BECOME AFFLICTED HIMSELF--
--AND ROT AWAY IN SECONDS.
NO TIME TO THINK, MARTYRS... ON YOUR MARK.
GET SET.

FZZZSHH
KOOOM!
RUN, YOU FOOLS.
FZZZSH
VWOOOSH

FZZZSSSSHH!

ARR!

JAY...

I'M REGAINING MUSCULAR CONTROL... TENDONS ARE TIGHT. LOOK, WE MAY HAVE TIME TO--

I DON'T THINK WE HAVE TIME TO DO ANYTHING, SON. ANYTHING BUT RUN.

WHAT HE DID TO WALLY... WE'VE GOT JUST MINUTES TO SAVE HIM AND THOSE PEOPLE--
--SO STEP BACK, GO TAKE CARE OF KADABRA AND LET ME TAKE THE LEAD. I'VE RUN MY RACE. I'LL TAKE THE HEAT HERE.
NO. I WON'T LET YOU DO THAT.
NO DISRESPECT, SUPERMAN.
BUT YOU DON'T HAVE A CHOICE.

FWWSSHHH!

REALLY?

YOU KNOW KADABRA IS TOYING WITH US. HE'S CONTROLLING EVERY MOVE THE FLASH IS MAKING. LIMITING HIS SPEED. IF HE WASN'T--
--WALLY WOULD'VE LEFT US IN THE DUST.
WHY DO THAT?
BECAUSE A RACE BETWEEN YOU AND ME IS MORE EVENLY MATCHED.
HE WANTS TO ENTERTAIN.
LISTEN TO ME FOR A SECOND, JAY. I'VE ALREADY ACTIVATED MY J.L.A. ALERT SIGNAL. WE'LL GET SOME HELP AND--
KADABRA IS A MASTER OF TECHNOLOGY, NOT MAGIC. CHANCES ARE HE'S JAMMED IT. IT'S ONLY YOU AND ME HERE.
THAT'S WHY I'M TELLING YOU AGAIN.
LET ME SAVE THESE PEOPLE.
I WON'T LET YOU SACRIFICE YOURSELF LIKE THAT, JAY.
MY GUESS IS I'LL BE MORE CAPABLE OF SURVIVING WHATEVER WALLY HAS BEEN INFECTED WITH THAN YOU.
AND MY GUESS IS THAT I WILL. I'M NOT GOING TO BET YOUR LIFE ON THIS, SUPERMAN.
BUT I'LL BET MINE.

FZZZSHH!
AAH.
I'M SORRY, SUPERMAN.

I... HATE... TO DO THIS. FEEL LIKE I'M CHEATING. IT'S SOMETHING WALLY'S BEEN... TRYING TO TEACH ME.
SAY GOOD-BYE TO YOUR SPEED.
NNNGH. WHAT ARE YOU--
I'M STEALING YOUR MOMENTUM, COMPOUNDING YOUR KINETIC ENERGY WITH MINE. GIVES ME A BOOST.
AND IT'LL SLOW YOU--
IT'S ABOUT TIME, OLD MAN. ABSORBING THE KRYPTONIAN'S SPEED.
WHAT?
NOW, LET'S EXTEND YOUR LITTLE LIGHTNING FIELD.
ABRA KADABRA.
KRRAAKOOMM
KRRAAKKLL

KRRKOOOOMMM
FWWOSSSH!

WHERE ARE WE?
FZZSSSHHH

HHH...
H-HE BROUGHT US BACK TO HIS *BIRTHPLACE*... A *TIME* OF *WAR* AND *NO FREE WILL*...

THE *Kaff* SIXTY-FOURTH CENTURY.
THEN, YOU'VE GOT A BETTER CHANCE OF GETTING BACK HOME WITH *WALLY*, SUPERMAN.
NO!
TELL JOAN...
KZZK
...I LOVE HER...
JAY!
DAMMIT, HE'S GOING INTO CARDIAC ARREST. THIS *CURSE*... IT'S--
IT'S *NOT* A *CURSE*.
I *SEE* IT NOW.

WHAT IS IT? WHAT DID YOU--
WHEN JAY TOUCHED YOU, MY MICROSCOPIC VISION SAW THE "CURSE" LEAP FROM YOUR BODY TO HIS. IT'S NOT MAGIC.
IT'S TECHNOLOGY.
NANO-TECHNOLOGY. MICROSCOPIC ROBOTS. BURROWING INTO JAY'S SKIN, ATTACKING HIS CELLS.
WZZZZZZ!
DAMMIT. WE'RE TRAPPED IN A WAR ZONE AND THE CLOSEST THING I HAVE TO A REAL FATHER... IS DYING.
WHY WOULD KADABRA WANT TO BRING US HERE ANYWAY?
OKAY. I'VE GOT AN IDEA.
I'M GOING TO TRIGGER JAY'S PHASING POWER. MAKE HIM IMMATERIAL.
IF I CAN VIBRATE HIM FAST ENOUGH, THE NANITES WON'T BE ABLE TO KEEP UP. THEY'LL REMAIN SOLID.
VZZZZZ!
LEAVING THEM VULNERABLE TO A BLAST OF MY HEAT VISION.
STAND BACK. THINGS ARE GOING TO GET HOT.
FZZZZ!

STEELWORKS
IMPLANT WEAPONS DIVISION 122
YII!
I DON'T MISS THIS TIME PERIOD.
THE ENDLESS FIGHTING, THE HOPELESS CONFORMITY... AND THE LACK OF ENTERTAINMENT.
HOWEVER I DO MISS THE AVAILABILITY OF... MAGICAL DEVICES.

FANTASTIC.
I NEEDED TO REPLENISH MY SUPPLY.

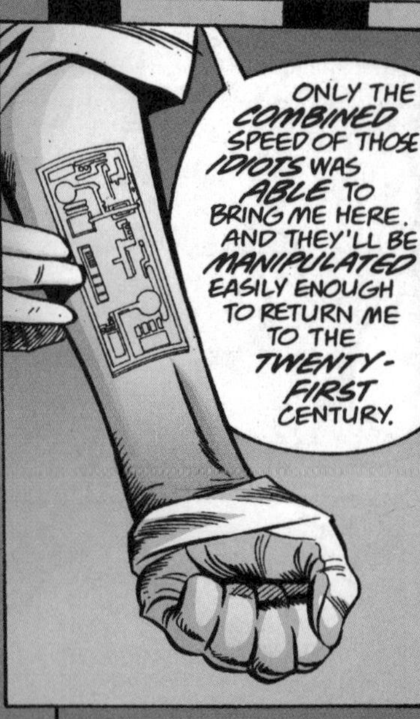
ONLY THE COMBINED SPEED OF THOSE IDIOTS WAS ABLE TO BRING ME HERE. AND THEY'LL BE MANIPULATED EASILY ENOUGH TO RETURN ME TO THE TWENTY-FIRST CENTURY.

KSSSSS!
UHNN! WHERE I WILL... AT LAST MAKE MY MARK IN HISTORY!

Fire.
ABRA KADABRA.

MAGNIFICEN--
FWOOSH

WOOOOOO

I COULD HEAR YOUR BRAVADO TWO BLOCKS AWAY.
GIVE IT UP, MANDRAKE.
YOU'RE IN MY WORLD, FLASH. DON'T YOU UNDER-STAND?
A WORLD WHERE ANYTHING YOU NEANDERTHALS EVER IMAGINED--
--IS MINE TO MAKE INTO REALITY!
Puppet.
ABRA KADABRA!
FWAKK!

ANYTHING.
VMMMMMMMMMM
SHAKKK!
YOU'RE ALL FINISHED, FLASH. PUT AWAY.
WITH THIS CHAOS CRYSTAL, I'LL BE ABLE TO ABSORB THE LIFE FORCE OF EVERYONE WITHIN FIVE HUNDRED MILES AND FIFTY-TWO CENTURIES.
I WILL MAKE EONS DISAPPEAR BEFORE YOUR EYES!
FOURTH DIMENSIONAL CHAOS SPHERES
ABRA KADA--

FZZZSHH
KWAANNG
GGG
SHAKK
KWANG
KWANG
KWANG
KWANG

KWANG
KWANG
KWANG
KWANG
KWANG

--BRA?
SHAKK
SHAKK

KRACKLE!

FWOOM!

WHAT? NO!

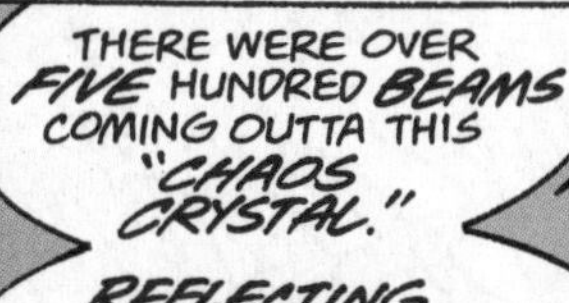
THERE WERE OVER FIVE HUNDRED BEAMS COMING OUTTA THIS "CHAOS CRYSTAL."
REFLECTING A THOUSAND MIGHT'VE BEEN DIFFICULT, BUT FIVE HUNDRED?

THAT'S JUST A JOG FOR ME, MAGICIAN.

KRAKOOM
YOU'RE SURE ABOUT THIS?
IT'S THE ONLY THING I CAN THINK OF. WALLY?
SUPERMAN'S RIGHT, JAY. WE'LL COMBINE OUR KINETIC ENERGY AND SPEED. AND WE'LL RIP RIGHT INTO THE TIME STREAM--
--AS MUCH AS I HATE IT.
BY FOCUSING ON OUR SIGNIFICANT OTHERS, WE'LL RETURN TO THE PROPER TIMELINE.
WHAT ABOUT THOSE "PEOPLE"? KADABRA'S "AUDIENCE." THEY WERE AGING AS FAST AS YOU--
WITH KADABRA CUT OFF FROM HIS POWER, HIS TELEKINETIC LINK TO THE NANITES IS GONE... RENDERING ALL HIS TRICKS INERT. THEY'LL BE FINE.
NOW KICK IT INTO HIGH GEAR, GUYS--
--AND LET'S GO HOME!
KOOOMMM
FWASSSHH!

EPILOGUE

That night.
I DON'T LIKE THIS PLACE.
NO ONE DOES, JAY.
BUT FOR NOW, THIS IS OUR BEST SOLUTION TO HOUSING THE ROGUES.
I ALMOST FEEL SORRY FOR HIM.
--TURN YOUR LIVER INTO JAM--
ALMOST.
I OWE YOU SOME THANKS, JAY. YOU WERE WILLING TO RISK YOUR LIFE FOR MINE.
SO WAS SUPERMAN, WALLY.
LOOK, SON. THAT'S THE BEAUTY OF WHO WE WORK WITH. IN THE JUSTICE SOCIETY AND THE JUSTICE LEAGUE.
ANY ONE OF US WOULD RISK OUR LIVES FOR ANOTHER. THAT'S WHAT REAL FRIENDS DO.
LIFE ISN'T PERFECT, AND IT CAN GET DOWN-RIGHT NASTY--
--BUT...WE SHOULDN'T EVER JUST GIVE UP..

Rathaway, Hartley AKA THE PIED PIPER
NO MATTER HOW DARK THINGS LOOK.

CHUK!

FWEEEEEEEEEEEEEEEEEEEEEEEEEEEEEEEF

EEE

EEE
EE

HE'S RIGHT, YOU KNOW...

IT'S GOOD TO HAVE FRIENDS.